Philosophical Introductions

Jürgen Habermas

Philosophical Introductions

Five Approaches to Communicative Reason

Introduction by Jean-Marc Durand-Gasselin

Translated by Ciaran Cronin

polity

Chapters 1–5 first published in German in *Philosophische Texte. Studienausgabe in fünf Bänden* © Suhrkamp Verlag, Frankfurt am Main 2009. All rights reserved and controlled through Suhrkamp Verlag Berlin

Introduction by Jean-Marc Durand-Gasselin © Suhrkamp Verlag Berlin, 2018

This English edition © Polity Press, 2018

Polity Press
65 Bridge Street
Cambridge CB2 1UR, UK

Polity Press
101 Station Landing
Suite 300
Medford, MA 02155, USA

ISBN-13: 978-1-5095-0671-2
ISBN-13: 978-1-5095-0672-9 (pb)

A catalogue record for this book is available from the British Library.

Library of Congress Cataloging-in-Publication Data

Names: Habermas, Jürgen, author.
Title: Philosophical introductions : five approaches to communicative reason / Jürgen Habermas.
Description: English edition. | Medford, MA : Polity, 2018. | Includes bibliographical references and index.
Identifiers: LCCN 2017059698 (print) | LCCN 2018015509 (ebook) | ISBN 9781509506750 (Epub) | ISBN 9781509506712 (hardback) | ISBN 9781509506729 (pbk.)
Subjects: LCSH: Philosophy, German--History--20th century. | Communication--Philosophy.
Classification: LCC B3258.H322 (ebook) | LCC B3258.H322 E5 2018 (print) | DDC 193--dc23
LC record available at https://lccn.loc.gov/2017059698

Typeset in 11 on 13 Sabon by Servis Filmsetting Ltd, Stockport, Cheshire
Printed and bound in Great Britain by Clays Ltd, Elcograf S.p.A.

The publisher has used its best endeavours to ensure that the URLs for external websites referred to in this book are correct and active at the time of going to press. However, the publisher has no responsibility for the websites and can make no guarantee that a site will remain live or that the content is or will remain appropriate.

Every effort has been made to trace all copyright holders, but if any have been inadvertently overlooked the publisher will be pleased to include any necessary credits in any subsequent reprint or edition.

For further information on Polity, visit our website: politybooks.com

Contents

Preface   vii

Introduction: The Work of Jürgen Habermas:
Roots, Trunk and Branches   1
Jean-Marc Durand-Gasselin

1. Foundations of Sociology in the Theory of
   Language   60

2. Theory of Rationality and Theory of Meaning   79
   I. Formal Pragmatics   80
   II. Communicative Rationality   86
   III. Discourse Theory of Truth   94
   IV. On Epistemology   99

3. Discourse Ethics   100
   I. Moral Theory   104
   II. On the System of Practical Discourses   114

4. Political Theory   122
   I. Democracy   129
   II. The Constitutional State   135
   III. Nation, Culture and Religion   137
   IV. Constitutionalization of International
       Law?   141

5. Critique of Reason   146
   I.   Metaphilosophical Reflections   151
   II. Postmetaphysical Thinking   156
   III. The Challenge of Naturalism   160
   IV. The Challenge of Religion   164

Notes   170
Index   212

Preface

On the occasion of my eightieth birthday, Suhrkamp Verlag encouraged me to make a systematic selection of essays on the five main areas on which my philosophical work has focused. I found this initiative very opportune because I have not written any books on important topics to which my philosophical interests, in the narrower sense, are directed. As a result, the individual collections of texts could take the place of unwritten monographs on:

- the foundations of sociology in the theory of language,
- the formal-pragmatic conception of language and rationality,
- discourse ethics,
- political philosophy, and
- the status of postmetaphysical thinking.[1]

The 'theory of communicative action' is so complex that it needs to be defended simultaneously on many different fronts. The foundations of such a social theory are laid down in 'preparatory studies' on philosophical questions, which must not be confused with social

---

[1] Jürgen Habermas, *Philosophische Texte*, 5 vols (Frankfurt am Main: Suhrkamp, 2009).

scientific questions; rather, they must be respected in their distinctive character. In the highly diverse network of scientific discourses, philosophical arguments can be defended only in the specific contexts in which the associated problems arise. The edition of philosophical essays was intended to throw light on this independent systematic import of philosophical questions. On the other hand, even though these attempts at explanation have to stand on their own two feet as contributions to technical philosophical discussions, at the same time they preserve their status within the more comprehensive context of an ambitious social theory.

In order to render this context transparent, I wrote an introduction to each of the five thematic volumes. In no other place have I attempted to provide an 'overview' of my philosophy, if I may speak in such terms, as a whole. For several decades I have had the vexing experience that, as our discipline becomes inexorably more specialized, my publications are no longer read as attempts to develop a philosophical conception as a whole. Rather than being read as a generalist's contributions to certain aspects of the theory of rationality or the theory of action, political theory or the theory of law, moral theory, language pragmatics or, specifically, social theory, they are interpreted in 'fragmented' form. This is why the synoptic view provided by these 'introductions' is close to my heart, without wishing to misrepresent their reference to a specific occasion of publication.

Publishing a series of introductions without the texts to which they refer is, of course, an imposition on the reader, who will if necessary have to track down these texts using the references.[2] Therefore, I am grateful to Jean-Marc Durand-Gasselin for fulfilling my all but impossible request to repair this deficiency. He

2   Citations of the texts discussed in the introductions are printed in **bold**.

supplements the introductions, which always refer to specific texts, with a masterful account of my approach from the perspective of a capable French colleague from across the Rhine.

Starnberg, December 2016
Jürgen Habermas

Introduction

The Work of Jürgen Habermas: Roots, Trunk and Branches

Jean-Marc Durand-Gasselin

The purpose of the present text is to introduce a collection of five essays by Jürgen Habermas, each of which originally served as an introduction to a thematic collection of philosophical articles on a single area of his work. To celebrate his eightieth birthday, Suhrkamp, Habermas's main German publisher, offered him the opportunity to devote a collection of articles to each of the most salient developments in his extremely prolific theoretical writings.[1] The volumes covered, in turn, the foundation of sociology in the theory of meaning, the relationship between rationality and the theory of meaning, discourse ethics, political theory and, finally, the critique of reason. Thus, the five introductory essays collected here offer an unusually rich and unparalleled overview of Habermas's theoretical construction and, taken together, provide an indispensable guide to the interpretation of his work.

However, these introductions also exhibit four characteristics that are apt to present difficulties for the reader, quite apart, of course, from their very rich intellectual content. The first and second difficulties are bound up with the fact that these are *thematic* introductions as well as being *philosophical* introductions in a rather academic sense of the term. Thus, they divide up Habermas's work along clear and fairly classical

1

institutional lines. However, this is at odds with the fact that, on the one hand, his work developed in a more organic way out of a central core and, on the other, its methodological point of departure was more interdisciplinary than this institutional division would suggest. A further difficulty is that Habermas tends to present *results* or *developments and elucidations* without explaining the underlying research process. Finally, the fourth difficulty is a direct implication of the first three: the introductions discuss articles that stem either from the 1970s (in a very few cases)[2] or from the 1980s to the present day (the majority), hence *from a period when Habermas's social theory had already been worked out*.[3]

In addition, I will try to throw light on these five thematic introductions by first (I) addressing the following four questions: To what extent do these texts refer to branches emanating from a single trunk or, alternatively, only to a single part of the trunk? In what sense was this trunk more interdisciplinary than these primarily philosophical and thematic surveys would suggest? In what ways, moreover, are the constituent problems and highly original intellectual forms that shaped the formulation of its major theoretical axes essential for understanding the Habermasian project? And, finally, to what extent does one part of the trunk, together with the roots, belong to the 1960s and even the 1950s? Then, in a second stage (II), I will discuss each of the introductions in turn, situating them within this project and its global dynamics of construction and elucidation.

I. General Traits of Habermas's Work

In this section I will sketch in very broad strokes Habermas's work as a whole and its theoretical construction since its inception.

A. Background, intentions and project

1. In order to comprehend the roots of the tree, several contextual elements must be borne in mind simultaneously. Here we must begin by *connecting* some of the contextual and historical elements which, for reasons of thematic presentation, occur *separately* in the different introductions where they are discussed for the most part in a preliminary way.

The emotional resonance of the first two – historical and political – elements is unequal, but they were both destined to play a leading role in Habermas's intellectual development. The first was the profound impact of the Second World War, the revelation of the horrors of Nazism and the project of re-education. The second was the context of the Federal Republic of Germany (FRG) during the post-war period of strong, technocratic economic growth, with its extremely narrow political spectrum restricted, on the right, by the Nazi past and, on the left, by the confrontation of the FRG with the communist German Democratic Republic (GDR). Habermas, who was born in Düsseldorf in 1929, embraced the project of re-education from the outset[4] and identified with the extra-parliamentary opposition and with the critique of the technocratic and Keynesian rationalization of the 1950s and 1960s. These two contextual elements combined from a very early date to imbue Habermas with a very stable system of suspicions and affinities concerning certain components of the German intellectual landscape of the 1950s and 1960s and, more generally, German intellectual history as a whole.

These suspicions and affinities would persist and *receive initial confirmation* within a specific academic context and through Habermas's early formative readings. Thus, these first two historical and political elements should be seen in relation to three features of the intellectual context properly speaking – namely, the structure of the German philosophical field and its major currents before and after Nazism, Habermas's reading of Karl Löwith's book *From Hegel to Nietzsche* and, finally, his encounter with Karl-Otto Apel.

In fact, the continuity of the German philosophical field before and after the war, with its inherent polarities and historical resonances, constitutes the first element, because the structure and the philosophical oppositions that marked this same field in the 1920s and 1930s were repeated, although in a *euphemized* way, after the war. The euphemization of the post-war philosophical field was the combined effect of the taboo on Nazism, the project of re-education, the new, extremely stable institutional system of the FRG and its confrontation with the GDR. Three families of ideas must be mentioned in this context. The first comprises four currents representing certain continuities and profound ambiguities within German philosophy – which, with its authoritarian and elitist traits, was generally politically conservative – before, during and after the Nazi period: the decisionist and expressionist Hobbesianism of Carl Schmitt and his followers; the philosophical anthropology of Erich Rothacker (Habermas's teacher in the 1950s), Helmuth Plessner and Arnold Gehlen; Martin Heidegger's phenomenology and its hermeneutic variant represented by Hans-Georg Gadamer; and Joachim Ritter's Right Hegelianism. These were the dominant currents in German academe in the post-war period and hence during Habermas's student years from 1949 to 1954.[5] The second family of ideas comprises the liberal rationalism of the proponents of the logical empiricism of the Vienna Circle who had been forced into exile, a current which was continued in a less rigid form by Karl Popper's critical rationalism, the main representatives of the Vienna School having remained in the United States. Finally, the third family constituted by German Marxism, whose Hegelian and Weberian traits were deeply influenced by Georg Lukács, found a continuation in the context of virulent anti-communism, reinforced by the confrontation with the GDR, with the return of the Frankfurt School and its colourful figures and interdisciplinary research. Habermas, who had been profoundly influenced by his youthful readings of Lukács's *History and Class Consciousness* and Horkheimer and Adorno's *Dialectic of Enlightenment*, would slip into the legacy of this third family of ideas and adopt in part the criticisms it addressed to the first two – a point of departure thematized in the five introductions.

Although Habermas initially identified with the revival of the German Marxist tradition, the euphemization of these oppositions would prompt him from a very early date to seek positions that *mediate between and combine* these three currents, something which would have been unthinkable in the 1930s, or even in the late 1920s, because of the extremism that was also reflected in the philosophical field. Thus, in the early 1960s, Habermas was already borrowing from all sides, in particular from Popper, Gadamer and the philosophical anthropology of the late Max Scheler.

Later, his reading of Karl Löwith's *From Hegel to Nietzsche*[6] would establish one of the keys to his interpretation of the history of philosophy in which Hegel marks the major caesura: on one side, metaphysical thought with its strong conception of theory and contemplative idea of reason as something separate from practice; and, on the other side, postmetaphysical thinking thrown into history, language and action, which recognizes its own fallibility and develops beginning with the generation of the Young Hegelians in particular.[7]

Finally, Apel played a considerable role in Habermas's intellectual development. Seven years his senior, a loyal friend and mentor and a conveyor of ideas, Apel introduced him to the European tradition of the philosophy of language, especially the hermeneutic tradition from Humboldt to Gadamer, but also to Wittgenstein, that is, to the linguistic turn. Finally, by familiarizing him with the American pragmatism of Charles Sanders Peirce, Apel also introduced Habermas to a tradition with a special affinity with the democratic project at the very moment in the 1950s and 1960s when a wind of change was blowing across the whole of the FRG from America as a result of re-education, strong economic growth and the geopolitics of the Cold War.[8] With this, the 'three turns' – the hermeneutic, linguistic and pragmatic turns – were already in place. In Germany and for Habermas, therefore, Apel played a major role in breaking down intellectual barriers and in formulating certain theoretical axes by reconciling traditions that had been separated by exile[9] (a reconciliation also facilitated by the euphemization evoked above), thus through the theme of turns and their convergence, but also through the central theme of communication conceived as a Peircean pragmatist recovery of Kantian themes.[10]

2. Let us now examine how these five elements are connected and form positive and negative intellectual polarities – polarities which would undergo incessant *ramification* and *justification* in the development of Habermas's work as a whole and which reflect, albeit in a modified way, the structure of the pre-war German philosophical field.

In the first place, we can identify critical polarities on two fronts. The first of these negative polarities is Habermas's critique – as a self-declared 'product of re-education' – of all intellectual continuities between the periods before and after National Socialism and, more generally, of anything which seemed to be an identifiable component of the intellectual prehistory of Nazism.[11] These include German Romanticism; the prophetic and aestheticizing posture; the esoteric and elitist

style; the obsession with ancient Greece and thus, more
generally, everything he would later subsume under
the heading of the 'German Platonic tradition' with its
ambivalence towards modernity;[12] the authoritarian-
ism and elitism that are at least in part expressions of
this tradition; and thus also even more generally the
forms of thought, both within and beyond Germany,
that exhibit a family resemblance with this conservatism
and Romanticism, in particular all forms of philosophical substantialism (concerning Being, the good, etc.)
that remain wedded to metaphysics. Although Apel's
influence tempered the severity of this retrospective
view,[13] it provides the background for understanding
Habermas's criticisms of Heidegger's and Schmitt's
young conservatism, of Gehlen's authoritarian insti-
tutionalism and Ritter's Right Hegelianism, not to
mention Gadamer's theory of understanding and prejudices and, finally, American neo-conservatism. But this
retrospective view also informed the critiques he would
later formulate of Hannah Arendt's neo-republicanism,
notwithstanding its affinity with his project, and of
American communitarianism – the former because of its
excessive reliance on the ancient model of republicanism, the latter because of its excessive indebtedness to
Aristotle. Finally, it is also from this point of view that
we must understand Habermas's reticence concerning
the aestheticizing and Romantic tendencies of Adorno,
Marcuse and Benjamin and concerning the French neo-
structuralists. Underlying this are the conflicts with
the 'German Platonic tradition' and its ambivalence
towards modernity.

Moreover, Habermas was critical of positivism in
its different forms because of its complicity with technocracy, its reduction of reason to calculation and its
tendency to reduce practical reason to an instrumental
dimension.[14] This is a guiding principle which also
informs his opposition to Popper's rationalism (already

apparent in the articles on the positivist dispute)[15] and
to the objectivism of Niklas Luhmann's systems theory
(although, for Habermas, the latter is also representative of paternalistic and technocratic conservatism) and,
more recently, his opposition to the reductionism of
neural materialism.

Secondly, we can identify a series of positive polarities. The first is the revival of the Hegelian and Weberian
tradition in German Marxism initiated by Lukács
and recast in Horkheimer's interdisciplinary Marxism.
Horkheimer himself was critical of the conservative
regressions of ontologism, as he was of positivism
and the reduction of philosophy to epistemology.[16]
Habermas also sought to revive the Kant of *What is
Enlightenment?* and the *Critique of Practical Reason*
and the Kantian notion of self-education through discussion, in opposition both to the aestheticism and
Romanticism of Schiller's *On the Aesthetic Education
of Man*, which found a partial continuation in Adorno,
Benjamin and Marcuse, and to substantialist and conservative ethical theories of the good. Another positive
polarity was the revival of the pragmatism of Peirce,
but also of Dewey, an emphatically democratic intellectual tradition, and, more directly, the antipositivist
tenor of the building blocks of the theory of communicative action, including the later Wittgenstein, Searle,
Toulmin, Schütz, Chomsky and Dummett, among
others, for the theory of communication, and Weber
and Parsons, among others, for social theory.

The first novelty here by comparison with Horkheimer
is the light Habermas casts on the positions he criticizes
and defends from the perspective of the historical and
intellectual caesura of the transition to a postmetaphysical era and of what took shape under Apel's influence
as the hermeneutic, pragmatic and linguistic turns,
even before the difference was thematized in terms of
the theory of communicative action per se. In addition,

Habermas's early reading of Löwith combined with Apel's work of intellectual importation to conceptualize the *delays* of ontologism, philosophical anthropology, substantialism and positivism within the vast undertaking of the *detranscendentalization* of reason and, symmetrically, of the need for Critical Theory to *adjust to this historical movement* by adapting itself to the hermeneutic, pragmatic and linguistic turns, precisely what would be accomplished by the theory of communicative action. The assumed continuation of Hegelian and Weberian Marxism from Lukács to Adorno is thus connected with a veritable *sequencing of the history of philosophy* that would inform the classification of theoretical materials for Habermas's own enterprise of a critical revival of German Marxism and for his critiques of the alternative positions: paradigm (philosophical ontology, modern philosophy of the subject, contemporary philosophy of language); turns (hermeneutic, pragmatic, linguistic); model ('logocentric' with the primacy of description, pluralistic).[17]

Viewed in a wider context, this sequencing of detranscendentalization must be related to the social theory that Habermas would develop during the 1960s and 1970s. The evolutionary process described by the theory of rationalization and of functional differentiation leads to the gradual emergence of distinct realms of social practice (science, politics, economics and art) supported by corresponding institutions (academies and universities, parliament and administrative bodies, the stock exchange and commercial courts, art schools, etc.) and inevitably transforms general and learned culture by differentiating intellectual disciplines (science and philosophy, science and theology, natural science and human science). Therefore, the delays or adjustments in the intellectual field also have a *sociological meaning* which is reflected in the Habermasian revival of the Marxist critique of ideology.

In addition to an immediate philosophical or intellectual dimension, therefore, the sequencing also has political overtones and a sociological correlate.

Finally, a second major difference from the first generation of Critical Theorists (which combines with detranscendentalization) is the communicative solution suggested by Apel's reading of Peirce, which led Habermas to differentiate between two 'paradigms' (but no longer primarily in a historical sense), the paradigm of the subject and the paradigm of intersubjectivity. Under the heading of 'logocentrism' (loosely inspired by Derrida), Habermas would develop a more discreet but nevertheless quite decisive critique of the undue primacy accorded by many theoretical approaches to the epistemic dimension of reason and the assertoric proposition over the moral or expressive dimensions of language, a primacy that is all the more likely to appear reductive under conditions of a differentiated modernity.

The result is a whole system of 'theoretical types' which enabled Habermas to construct and understand his own position and those of his protagonists and underlies his extraordinary theoretical productivity.

3. This sequencing also informs a modus operandi which proceeds by identifying *overlaps* and *convergences* in the theoretical materials classified and selected in accordance with the sequence, a reflection of the fact that the postmetaphysical philosopher lacks any privileged intuitions or intellectual instruments of his or her own.[18] The overlaps in question serve as *hermeneutic and heuristic guides* for construction *in combination with standard conceptual and empirical arguments*.[19] Thus the theory of communicative action will both be inscribed in this sequence and embody this modus operandi. This applies, albeit in more or less explicit ways, to social theory, legal theory, ethics and the theory of reference.

The sequencing and modus operandi in question express within the philosophical field, each in its own way, the problem of German backwardness and that of a *catch-up revolution*. The latter term crops up throughout Habermas's work: it can be found in his social theory and in all the developments on the theory of reason and truth, as well as in his moral theory and theory of law. Ultimately, it depicts the German case, with its National Socialist regression and the associated forms of legitimation, as one of arrested development and anti-modern regression.

Faith in modernity restored

But, as we shall see, Habermas would also have to find solutions for *particular problems*. This is why many of his texts take the form of *problematized inventories* of different theories classified according to their relevance for the movement of detranscendentalization and according to the answers they provide to problems formulated by Habermas within this movement.

Viewed as a whole, therefore, these elements mark out an emotional, intellectual and philosophical framework which Habermas would *spell out progressively* over a period of more than thirty years between the 1950s and the 1980s and within which the construction of his original *project* of a critical revival of the Frankfurt heritage must be situated.

4. Habermas's work in Frankfurt, where he was recruited as Adorno's research assistant in 1956,[20] was initially concerned with the political opinions of students.[21] Already in the introduction to this collaborative study he evokes a combative conception of the public arena and civic participation. Thus, the critical question of *depoliticization* through technocratic politics and of the historical and intellectual substance of democracy tended to supplant Adorno's problem of conformism at the top of the young Habermas's intellectual agenda, reflecting his primary affiliation with critical Marxism coupled with his experience of re-education which

marked the generational difference from the older representatives of the Frankfurt School. Indeed, Habermas felt that, from the end of the 1950s onwards, the first generation had not developed the necessary theoretical means to comprehend the normative substance of democracy and hence the historical relevance of the project of re-education.[22] Moreover, this generation had failed to produce a genuine sociological and philosophical theoretical framework for its enterprise, with the result that the interdisciplinary work had ultimately become peripheral or subordinate, with Adorno and Horkheimer developing their thought in an aphoristic and personal style.[23]

Thus, Habermas wanted to reconstruct the theoretical core of Horkheimer's Hegelian and Weberian Marxism taking the public sphere and public opinion as his guide and by drawing on materials whose theoretical force and historical and hermeneutical relevance he was beginning to conceptualize and justify based on his reading of Löwith and the perspectives of Apel, as well as on perspectives borrowed from the protagonists of an intellectual field which had been pacified in part (Gadamer, Popper). The realization of this project would be his main preoccupation from the late 1950s until the publication of the *Theory of Communicative Action*. It constitutes the base of the trunk from which the tree would grow and subsequently branch out.

B. *Problems, materials and solutions*

1. For Habermas it was imperative to make a detailed preliminary analysis of the aspects of history to which Marx's theory was blind and hence which pre-programmed both the failure of Marxist predictions and the pessimism of the entire Hegelian and Weberian Marxist tradition from Lukács to Adorno, not to mention the brutality of Leninism. What was called for,

therefore, was a different history of modernity from that of Marxism which would highlight the latter's theoretical blind spots. Here we can see all the developments mentioned above taking shape together with the *philosophical problems* with which Habermas would have to deal.

This alternative history was developed in Habermas's book on the transformation of the public sphere,[24] a continuation of the study on the political attitudes of students that was written under the supervision of Wolfgang Abendroth.[25] In this work, Habermas develops a genealogy of democratic institutions by tracing their organic links with the emergence of the public sphere and the associated forms of sociability based on critical discussion. Democratic life depends on the degree of commitment and participation by the citizens in public deliberations.[26] It was initially promoted by the rise of the educated urban bourgeoisie discussing issues related to art and economics in clubs, cafés and salons, and it inspired certain central institutional reforms of the revolutionary period including that of parliament. Then, as democracy became generalized in the first half of the nineteenth century, it was confronted with the question of education and of the electoral franchise, and subsequently, from the final third of the nineteenth century up to the present day, with the rise of conformist mass culture and the technocratic state. Each of these factors contributed in its own way to reducing the democratic potential of the public arena and gave rise to a specific form of anomie whose main symptom is depoliticization.[27]

The blind spots are also illuminated by a history of social philosophy whose task is to show what Marx inherited.[28] Here we can see how Habermas tried to combine the requirement of fallibility with the hermeneutic dimension, while remaining true to his critical intention, in a kind of programmatic encompassing of Popper's and Gadamer's positions, starting from social theory and from the historical caesura between meta-physics and postmetaphysics underlined by Löwith.[29] Thus, Marxism appears to have worked with a model of social action that is too close to instrumental action. This perspective can be traced back at least as far as Machiavelli and is at the root of the inability of Marxism to account for how democracy combines with the redistribution facilitated by technological progress to stabilize capitalism from the final third of the nine-teenth century onwards. And this same model explains the Leninist tendencies towards brutality within the Marxist movement. Marx failed to take advantage of the byways pursued by Vico, who criticized the sub-sumption of human practice under the model of natural science, or to learn from the eighteenth-century Scottish, or later the Kantian, philosophy of public opinion.[30] Moreover, Marx had an excessively positivistic under-standing of his own work, being incapable of attaching a specific epistemological status to this project of a theory that seeks to emancipate practice.

For Habermas, the clarification of the dimension of the understanding of practice called for a richer model, or models, of social action which take up the ideas of Vico and the philosophy of public opinion, using the new theoretical tools imported notably by Apel (Peirce and the later Wittgenstein). Only in this way could both the stabilization of capitalism and its specific patholo-gies (depoliticization, mass culture and technocracy) be comprehended, but without renouncing the scientific standard of fallibilism. Moreover, the original epistemo-logical profile of Marxism also had to be rethought in order to clarify the status of a predictive science whose characteristics presuppose both the explanation of the tendencies exhibited by its object and the interested understanding of its possible emancipation.

These constitute the two axes of the project of con-struction that took shape in the early 1960s. They correspond to separate publications but nevertheless form a loop.[31]

2. In *On the Logic of the Social Sciences* and *Technik und Wissenschaft als Ideologie*,[32] which correspond to the first axis, Habermas collects theoretical materials and sketches the overall physiognomy of his future theory, but without reaching satisfactory solutions, something he would arrive at only in the early 1970s.

In the first text, which in typical Habermasian fashion takes the form of a *problematized inventory* (see I.B.3), Weber's theory of ideal types, Wittgenstein's theory of language games, G.H. Mead's social behaviourism, Alfred Schütz's social phenomenology and Talcott Parsons's functionalism (that is, the schema comprising the four functions Adaptation, Goals, Integration and Latency [abbreviated in what follows as 'AGIL'] and the epistemology of frames of reference) are cited as theoretical means for addressing the *comprehensive dimension of practice* without renouncing the *predictability requirements of fallibilism*, and hence also as the means of avoiding an instrumental opposition between *theory* and *practice*. Thus, there emerges, in a kind of theoretical combination, a historically informed functionalist programme that deals with communicative practice and its lived and critical or emancipatory dimensions. But it remains impossible to specify precisely what role is played by this communicative practice in history and society.

In the second text, the dualistic character of social theory (instrumental and strategic action, on the one hand, and communicative action, on the other, typified as in Weber) is projected onto the scale of universal history with the respective extension and development of these two types of action in the three phases of humanity (also typified) – namely, primitive society, traditional hierarchical society and modern society. Taking primitive society as his point of departure,

Habermas hypothesizes that instrumental and strategic action were at first only weakly developed within the context of a pervasive, enveloping mythology. Then he describes a kind of gradual expansion of instrumental and strategic action, but still within the limits of a sufficient legitimation of traditional forms of statutory hierarchy. And, finally, during the modern era, the extension of instrumental action and the erosion of myth call for a higher level of communicative coordination, as is shown by the emergence of the public sphere. However, this form of coordination is impeded by the simultaneous development of technocratic rationality and mass culture.

Modern public sphere a response to erosion of traditional modes of communicative action?

We will come across the combination of these materials with this dynamic outline again, but in a more satisfactory and more developed form, in the interdisciplinary studies from Habermas's tenure at the Starnberg Institute between 1971 and 1981. But in order to achieve this synthesis, he would first have to develop a satisfactory theory of communication.

In *Knowledge and Human Interests*,[33] which corresponds to the second axis, Habermas presents the historical part of his epistemological project of founding the different types of discourse in distinct anthropological interests. He distinguishes three types of interests (instrumental, hermeneutic and critical) corresponding to three types of scientific knowledge (nomological, historical and critical). And to this corresponds the dichotomy of the types of actions: the nomological sciences informed by an instrumental interest refer to instrumental or strategic action, whereas the hermeneutic and critical sciences both refer to interaction. In this way Habermas shows how, from Kant to Freud, via Dilthey, Peirce and Mach, the various philosophies of knowledge sought to elaborate such a plural epistemology, but failed to do so because of the unitary or positivist presuppositions of their respective theoretical frameworks. Habermas would abandon this project in the early 1970s when the first axis absorbed the second, in particular, as we shall see, through his reconstructive epistemology.

3. The solution to the problem posed in *On the Logic of the Social Sciences* is presented in the Christian Gauss Lectures, which Habermas delivered at Princeton in 1971.[34] This is why it appears as the first chapter of the first volume of the *Studienausgabe*: it provides the foundation on which everything else is built. In these lectures, Habermas addresses what seemed to him to be the solution he had sought in vain in *On the Logic of the Social Sciences* – namely, a theory of linguistic communication that makes it possible to understand both the symbolically structured character of the lifeworld and its reproduction over time, and how social agents can thematize and provide a partial, critical elucidation of this lifeworld in reasoned discourse.

In order to develop such a theory, Habermas had to show that verbal communication represents a specific competence involving *speech acts* (Searle), the observance and *comprehension* of rules (Wittgenstein), *argumentative resources* (Toulmin) and a *lived* dimension (Schütz), using a *reconstructive* Chomskian epistemological model transposed to the level of universal pragmatics that is able to describe the rules of agreement. Reasoned discourse relates to one of the segments of the lifeworld and provides a *local clarification* of this segment in the rules of verbalized agreement. Hence this clarification presupposes that the partners obey rules of acceptability as a precondition for reaching agreement. In other words, if they did not respect these rules, they would not be able to take seriously the reasons they invoke to justify their respective *claims to validity*. The *claims to validity implicitly* raised by the different types of speech acts in everyday interaction have to be *explained and justified* with reasons when, in the absence of automatic accord, agreement must be restored through discussion. To this corresponds a consensual theory of truth, according to which truth is the claim to validity raised by a constative speech act in the context of its justification, that is, in discourse. Habermas would draw on Dummett's theory of justified assertability in particular, integrating and generalizing it to all claims to validity and the corresponding speech acts, starting from the case of assertoric propositions, in order to provide a kind of discursive, postmetaphysical version of Kant's three *Critiques*.[35] Then he would have to construct a whole grammar of the use of personal pronouns to account for learning and the rule-governed mobilization of reasons to support our claims to validity.[36]

In fact, this reconstructive epistemology would both complicate the project of *Knowledge and Human Interests* – because the level of the claims to validity of speech acts is difficult to reconcile with the more transcendental level of the constitution of object domains defended by the project of cognitive interests – and render it superfluous – because the reconstructive epistemological model seems sufficiently ambitious to be able to dispense with an additional anthropology of knowledge interests. It also became superfluous as a result of the waning influence of what had originally been its main adversary, namely the positivist paradigm (Quine, Kuhn, etc.). This was also the moment at which Habermas developed a progressively more systematic critique of his own tradition. *Knowledge and Human Interests* now seemed to him to be too wedded to the pathos of the philosophical anthropology that had marked his philosophical training and to defend too strong a notion of self-reflection, understood as the activity of a subject on the scale of a people or a social class, and of the theorist, understood accordingly as a kind of psychoanalyst of this subject writ large. These are the most important reasons why Habermas abandoned this project.[37]

4. At the same time, what is striking about these two projects, even before Habermas thematized it himself in the early 1980s, is that they share the same modus operandi and mode of theorizing, which resonates profoundly with the rejection of any privileged philosophical intuition, with its prophetic connotations and affinities with the German Platonic tradition. Thus, both projects involve a problematized inventory of theoretical materials coupled with a hermeneutic tracing of these same materials over a given period and the cutting and pasting justified by a local debate involving detailed discussion while at the same time aiming to produce a comprehensive theory.

C. Puzzle of the frame of reference, complementary hypotheses, critical fronts

1. In the early 1970s, around the time he left Frankfurt for the Max Planck Institute in Starnberg, therefore, Habermas was in a position to extend the construction of the frame of reference, which he had merely outlined in *Technik und Wissenschaft als Ideologie*, to enable him to take account of the dialectic of the public sphere, starting from the solution he developed in the Gauss Lectures.

Here I will present the principles informing this construction that are indispensable for understanding his work as a whole. It is at this point that the challenge of constructing the puzzle becomes especially clear, namely to integrate the elements cut and pasted from theories derived from distinct horizons into a whole and thereby render them *metatheoretically coherent*, while seeking to reconstruct intuitions and everyday practices (whose history Habermas recounted in his book on the public sphere) *in a perpendicular manner*. This will throw light on the structure of constructive works such as the

Theory of Communicative Action or *Between Facts and Norms*, but also, albeit more indirectly, on the constructive character of Habermas's moral theory and his theory of reference.

As mentioned briefly above, Habermas borrowed the epistemology of frames of reference from Parsons as a means of conceptualizing the typified functional articulations of the structure of society as a whole (namely, the four AGIL functions and the three elements of the lifeworld: culture, institutions and personality structure) and its dynamic process (the three systematized periods – primitive society, hierarchical society organized around the state and modern society – referring to ideal-typical moments of functional differentiation). A frame of reference is a set of typified concepts that must be made coherent in their interrelations in order to have theoretical points of reference that are sufficiently salient to capture reality. Therefore, Habermas's first task was to establish a connection between communicative competence and this dynamic functional differentiation. What was required was a theory capable of explaining how and why communicative action both develops and is impeded at each of these three stages. This involved a set of constructive tasks that would constitute the intellectual core of Habermas's project during the 1970s, notably *Legitimation Crisis*,[38] *Zur Rekonstruktion des Historischen Materialimus*[39] and, finally, the *Theory of Communicative Action*.

The most straightforward approach is to discuss them beginning with the Parsonian categories explicitly taken up by Habermas. The first requirement was to develop a theory of communicative competence and its development towards maturity at the level of the *individual personality* and to show that it undergoes development and can be impeded. This is the role played by Habermas's reference to the social psychology of Mead and to Kohlberg's psychological theory of stages of moral development according to which the self structures its motivations in a progressively more general way by adopting the perspective of a progressively more abstract generalized Other, and this increase in generality can be understood as a process of learning in stages.[40]

Then Habermas had to show how progress or regress at the level of *institutions* can be conceived as being mediated by socially diffused practices of argumentation in connection with *culture* and its transformations. This he achieved by using the psychology of learning as a heuristic guide on a historical scale to show in what ways institutions are more or less general or abstract, following a classical Durkheimian approach, where these collective learning processes presuppose *occasional causes* that prompt learning. In this way, one can conceive of mechanisms that disseminate or inhibit deliberative participation on a social scale and, at a dynamic level, on an evolutionary and historical scale. In addition, Habermas had to show how *culture* necessarily diffracts by stages in the evolutionary dynamic into scientific, aesthetic, axiological and normative culture, where these different elements by contrast are fused together in the enveloping myth of primitive society. This dynamic ultimately compels linguistic interactions to follow this differentiation, at least in part.

Finally, Habermas had to connect this with *functional differentiation* in order to show that the process of *functional differentiation of the AGIL functions* (i.e., Adaptation: economics; Goals: politics; Integration: society; Latency: culture) in three typified stages ('primitive' society, hierarchical society and modern society) dictates that *individual communicative competences*, *institutions* and *culture* exhibit a certain level of learning at each stage. In particular, communicative competences and institutions, as we have just seen, must exhibit a certain level of abstraction and culture a certain degree of differentiation (especially between expressive-evaluative components, the scientific descriptive components and the normative components). In this way we can understand the centrality of communicative action in the dynamic of evolution, because it performs the three functions of cultural transmission, the coordination of action and socialization that cannot be performed by instrumental or strategic action. Thus, Habermas can account for the role played in differentiated and rationalized modern societies by the deliberative clarification of our reasons for acting and thinking.

On the other hand, against the functionalism of Parsons, especially in Luhmann's exaggerated objectivist version, Habermas also had to show that the detour via claims to validity (i.e. via consciousness, criticism and language, precisely what social behaviourism, the theory of learning and formal pragmatics enable us to conceptualize) was necessary in the evolutionary dynamic and therefore that the adjustment of the personality, social and cultural components of the lifeworld was by no means automatic in comparison to functional differentiation. The latter is precisely Luhmann's claim, because it would justify on the one hand methodological objectivism, and on the other a technocratic, paternalistic and conservative approach to social problems.[41] This is why the theory of learning and of occasional causes connected with claims to validity would not render completely superfluous Habermas's journalistic writings which sought to encourage historical learning and highlight potentially regressive implications of particular policies or events. This challenge would be taken up by the *Kleine politische Schriften* once the theory had been established. Habermas thus anticipated a division of theoretical and critical labour between his major theoretical works and his interventions as a publicist, which became much more numerous from the 1980s onwards.

From this point of view, the work exhibits a complete background theoretical unity.

Thus, in the communicative process, the different claims to validity, which are at first virtually conflated in the at once cognitive, normative and expressive transmission of myth, undergo a partial differentiation in the evolutionary dynamic, necessitated by the functional differentiation of the social functions (AGIL) and of the corresponding evolution of the dimensions of the lifeworld (personality, society and culture). The different claims to validity tend to embody complementary but distinct dimensions of modernity: the claim to epistemic validity is embodied in institutionalized science, the claim to normative correctness in morality and law and the claim to expressive truth in art.

Three types of social integration thus become differentiated: the global functional integration (AGIL) rendered more and more difficult by social evolution, which is a process of differentiation; systemic integration which presupposes the development of the media of money and power in the economy and bureaucratic administration (A and G); and social integration through language and solidarity in institutions (I) and through the resources of culture (L). In differentiated modern society, therefore, there may be competition within the two types of media (money [or the market]/ power [or bureaucracy]) and between systemic integration and social integration, which mark out political alternatives, as we shall see below.

2. Starting from this *fully typified and systematized* frame of reference, Habermas could *add* all of the *necessary complementary hypotheses* to his sociological and critical work, just as he could for the reconstructive method of universal pragmatics and later for law, as we shall see below with reference to the first and fourth introductions (see II.A.3 and especially II.D.2). But *already* at this first level, the dialectic of the public

sphere appears to be a contradictory effect, on the one hand, of the increased demand for argumentative coordination of modern or postconventional, functionally differentiated society and, on the other hand, of the short-circuiting of this argumentative coordination by the combined powers of the market and the technocratic state, which seeks to compensate for and correct the effects of this same market. These powers are magnified considerably by this same functional differentiation, which assumes the forms of a bureaucratic treatment of social problems, of a purely monetary mediation of social interaction or of a mass culture that disseminates factitious and passive identificatory models. All three forms of functional differentiation impede deliberative coordination and lead to a regression of postconventional personality structures on a social scale or they impede learning at the level of personality structures by keeping them at the conventional level. But Habermas could plan in a *programmatic* way a whole series of *additional* complementary hypotheses to explain more local or more specific situations.

3. From the early 1970s[42] onwards, therefore, but even more exhaustively in the early 1980s, Habermas could present an organic picture of the dialectics of organized modernity with the major synthesis of the *Theory of Communicative Action*. Modernity, he argued, is animated, on the one hand, by a democratic thirst for inclusion and deliberation bound up with the collapse of the conventional culture of hierarchical and traditional society, and therefore corresponds to the postconventional level of learning required by personalities, institutions and culture. On the other hand, it is driven by criticism of the (conservative) forms of conventional culture and of the systems of money and power (technocracy, mass culture) that impede the development of this deliberative cooperation. This thirst is reflected in particular by the student, feminist

and environmental social movements, which represent trends opposed to mass culture and to technocratic or economic domination. This picture took polemical aim at – especially American but soon after also European – neo-conservatism which, in a triple reaction against the welfare state, the student, civil rights and 'sexual minorities' social movements and the stagflation of the 1970s, argued that forms of regulation by the welfare state should be replaced by market-based mechanisms. Since the mid-1970s, the weakening of 'positivism', as we have seen, and the 'crisis of the welfare state' had shifted the focus of criticism towards neo-conservatism. But criticism also had to be directed against the pessimism of the first-generation Frankfurt School, which was too closely allied with the ambivalence of Romanticism and German idealism towards modernity.

Thus, Habermas could conclude this work with a whole *programme* of research with which, thanks to the detranscendentalized and intersubjectivist frame of reference of this new theory, he was able to 'rejuvenate' the diagnoses of the first generation of the Frankfurt School.

4. Somewhat paradoxically, this brings to an end the first period of Habermas's work, namely the revival or recasting of the Hegelian and Weberian tradition within German Marxism, extending from Lukács to first-generation Critical Theory. By resigning the directorship of the Max Planck Institute in Starnberg in the early 1980s, which had provided him with an ideal environment for developing his interdisciplinary and critical perspectives, and returning to a more classical position as professor of philosophy and sociology in Frankfurt, which he held until his appointment as emeritus professor in 1994, Habermas left behind a huge critical and very ambitious constructive project that he would go on to realize only *in part*. He would pursue new intellectual agendas that led him to develop his theory in new

directions, engaging with new protagonists for whom Marxist critical culture was not the central issue, at the very moment when the American intellectual field achieved a position of unprecedented dominance.

D. Elucidations, developments and readjustments

1. Most of the texts selected by Habermas for inclusion in the *Studienausgabe* and discussed in the introductions contained in the present volume date from the early 1980s to the present day. This period is marked by a threefold movement: first, by Habermas's retrospective philosophical *elucidation* of the foundations of the theory of communicative action, in particular the thematization of postmetaphysical thinking with its constitutive hermeneutic, pragmatic and linguistic turns[43] (see below II.A.1 and especially II.E.1 and 2) and of possible relations between philosophy and religion (see II.E.3);[44] secondly, by his *development* of a moral theory and a theory of law as a further elaboration of the theory of communication (see II.C and II.D);[45] and, finally, by his self-critical re-examination of certain basic assumptions of his theory, especially for the theory of law and of the relations between truth and justification[46] (see II.D and II.B.3). In addition to purely theoretical works, Habermas produced a wealth of political writings connected with German national controversies (the historians' debate, Germany's place in the construction of Europe, etc.) and international current affairs (the construction of the European Union, US foreign policy),[47] as well as intermediate writings in which he responds to potentially profound transformations of contemporary societies (the destiny of the nation-state,[48] eugenics,[49] neural materialism[50] [see II.E.2] and the place of religion[51] [see II.E.3]). The latter writings deal with the historical relationships between learning and occasional causes and constitute the special preserve of his journalistic observations and interventions.

This is where Habermas's work opens itself up to agendas besides that of reconstructing the Hegelian and Weberian Marxism of Critical Theory in terms of the theory of communicative action, which dominated the first period. The two agendas that dominated Habermas's writings during the 1980s were, on the one hand, the modernism/postmodernism debate, which had very different resonances on either side of the Atlantic, and, on the other, the multiple responses to John Rawls's work in moral and legal theory. In the wake of the postmodernism debate, the question of a new form of scepticism associated especially with Richard Rorty led Habermas to revisit his theory of reference in the mid-1990s. In the wake of the reception of Rawls, but also of more local or political debates (on constitutional patriotism, the European constitution and criticism of American foreign policy), Habermas's theory of morality and his theory of law led him to defend a multidirectional politics of learning and of discursive proceduralism, as can be seen in the 1990s and 2000s.

2. However, because the three movements of elucidation, development and readjustment occurred in the context of new agendas that in part overshadow the Hegelian and Marxist legacy, commentators have often assumed that they represent a reorientation of Habermas's thought (specifically, in a Kantian, normative direction). But in fact they were primarily the result of a *local thematization* of his own frame of reference and of taking Kant as a reference point in these academic debates in European intellectual history,[52] while the basic thrust of his thought remained in essence the same and preserved its critical potentials.[53] This is why the texts selected for the *Studienausgabe* and Habermas's introductions have a more academic and less interdisciplinary and critical tone than his work as a whole and the theory per se. The academic tone is the combined result of his having completed a cycle

of theoretical development, his return to an academic post and, above all, as noted above, the new agendas in which he elucidates, develops and readjusts his theory in a global intellectual context henceforth dominated by the American field.

3. It should now be apparent how the organic growth of Habermas's theory and, more generally, the vast dynamic constructive project of his work should be divided up into phases. There was an initial phase dating from the late 1950s and the 1960s during which the problems to be solved took shape, followed by a constructive phase, accelerated dramatically with the Gauss Lectures for the reasons we have seen; then, having accomplished the mission of renewing the theoretical core and critical programme of Critical Theory, there followed a phase of elucidation pointing in different directions (on reason in general, moral philosophy, later the philosophy of law and the theory of meaning) that are less concerned with sociology and more with normative political theory.

Formulated in terms of the organic metaphor of a tree: the roots (detranscendentalization and the three turns) were present from the outset but became explicit only in the 1980s; the trunk of social construction was elaborated in part during the 1960s but especially in the period 1971–81; and then the branches (reason, moral, law) developed from the 1980s onwards. The developments that are closer to simple elucidation – the smallest branches, as it were, such as those on the relationship to science or religion – date from the 1990s and 2000s. The political writings that accompanied the whole development of Habermas's work, and which on this metaphor represent the foliage, also became especially abundant from the 1980s onwards.

4. This caesura in the early 1980s also has a bearing on the form assumed by Habermas's theoretical work. In the first phase of his work, he was clearly guided by

theoretical *convergences* that led him to affirm *strong forms of symmetry* between the different claims to validity in his theory of communication; during the second phase, under the constraint of debates that exhibit a certain autonomy, he re-examined some of these symmetry effects. This will become especially apparent when we examine his distinction between truth and justification and the difference at the level of validity claims between truth and rightness. The second period is marked by four essential readjustments: first, in his theory of the relations between truth and justification, truth could no longer be reduced to the justified assertability of claims to validity (see II.B.3); second, regarding rationality, the relationship between communicative rationality and instrumental and epistemic rationality was in need of clarification (see II.B.3); third, with regard to the discourse principle, its roles in morality versus law had to be differentiated (see II.C.2); and, finally, regarding law, it was associated less closely with the medium of power and its central functional and normative significance for modernity became apparent (see II.D). I will address these adjustments directly in the presentation of each of the introductions and of more technical developments.

II. A Brief Overview of Habermas's Introductions

Habermas's aim in the five collections of articles constituting the *Studienausgabe* was to bring together what seemed to him in retrospect to be his contributions to different fields of philosophy. Thus, together they formed a kind of unwritten book, one which was as systematic as such an unwritten work could be. My aim in what follows is to shed light on these contributions to philosophy starting from the genesis and structure of the social theory we have just discussed, thus following the same procedure as Habermas in his introductions to each of the collections.

To anticipate, using the organic image of a tree and picking up the thread of what we have said: the first and fifth introductions discuss both the trunk of social theory and the roots of detranscendentalization and, as we have just seen, form a loop;[54] the second, third and fourth introductions address the main branches of the theory of reason, ethics and the theory of law. Finally, the second part of the fifth introduction discusses the secondary branches dealing with the relationship between modern reason and science, on the one hand, and religion, on the other. Through these five introductions, therefore, we can trace the organic development of Habermas's philosophical thought, bearing in mind that, as mentioned at the beginning and shown in the first part, his intellectual work as a whole cannot be reduced to this specifically philosophical contribution. Thus, we will follow the order of the introductions in discussing how the central philosophical concepts and themes are deployed in these introductory texts.[55]

A. Claim to validity, reconstruction and modernity

The central challenge facing Habermas was first to show that a theory of society must be based on rule-governed linguistic interaction and on a reconstructive epistemology. Thus the central concepts of his theory, which cut across all of the philosophical developments on reason, morality and law, are justified here at the level of social theory.[56] For this purpose, the first requirement was to demonstrate the theoretical force of the model of communicative action by comparison with other forms of social action, then to indicate its lateral connections with the theory of individual social competence and with society and, finally, to highlight the originality of the reconstructive epistemology that informs it. Finally, in conclusion, its consequences for our conception of modernity had to be clarified, a central philosophical and sociological concern of Habermas's theory. I will discuss these aspects in turn, following Habermas's procedure in the first introduction.[57]

1. Habermas recalls the importance of the Gauss Lectures[58] in providing a *solution* to the *problems* that became explicit from *The Logic of the Social Sciences* onwards and are marked by an anti-positivist stance, namely, as we saw above, the problem of the 'explanation' of 'understanding' and that of 'theory and practice'. The symbolic dimension of social action must be 'understood' in the sense of hermeneutics; but, in order not to lose sight of the requirement of scientificity (or the dimensions of predictability and fallibilism or of 'explanation'), the rules of production of this symbolic dimension have to be thematized. Moreover, the theorist is not dealing with a neutral object to which a theory can be applied in an external, instrumental or technical manner, but is instead theorizing a practice that he or she can help to transform.[59]

We have already discussed the construction of the solution above: the speech act is the medium of communication by which the speaker and the hearer are supposed to establish both an appropriate communicative relationship between themselves *and* a relationship with what the speaker is talking about (a fact, a state of affairs). *Communicative competence* is conceived as the ability to master a system of rules permitting us specifically to produce well-formed speech acts in the sense of the twofold normative relation to others and to the world. In this way, Habermas can conceive of a system of rules of communication that crosscuts the different speech acts and shapes their illocutionary forces. Speech acts are the bearers of the *claims to validity* addressed by the speaker to a hearer aimed at reaching agreement on a state of affairs, where these claims can be made explicit and are open to justification if agreement does not arise automatically.

2. Next, Habermas has to show the organic connections between universal pragmatics and the rest of the theory by proceeding from the most general considerations to critical and constructive considerations. He first discusses the theoretical strengths of communicative action compared to the other major models of action (i.e. strategic action, normatively regulated action and dramaturgical action): communicative action *includes each of the aspects described* by these competing theories precisely because human verbal communication contains the different claims to validity (epistemic, normative and expressive) and, functionally speaking, it must allow the reproduction of the lifeworld over time.

Thus, Habermas can explain the connection between universal pragmatics and the lifeworld and the social order in general, which enables him to provide a version of universal pragmatics oriented to history and to the critique of Parsonian functionalism, a solution highlighted in *The Logic of the Social Sciences* and developed in the Gauss Lectures.[60] Indeed, the social coordination of ego and alter tends to vary between two extremes: at the one extreme, immediate coordination with verbal exchanges reduced to a minimum because the cultural resources, legitimacy of institutions and personality structures – i.e. the components of the *lifeworld* – are shared, there being a maximum of virtually automatic consensus; at the other extreme, problematized coordination presupposing rule-governed verbal clarification and discussion of the elements of culture or legitimacy apt to promote learning. This is why between these two extreme forms we must keep in mind the theory of learning developed by Habermas in the 1970s and its connection with the social and historical dynamics of functional differentiation, as we saw above. But, as Habermas points out at the very end of the introduction to this text, we must also keep in mind the goals

of the theoretical reformulation of the critical themes
of the first-generation Frankfurt School thanks to the
Parsonian theory of power and money as necessary
functional intermediaries of a differentiated society that
short-circuit deliberative coordination and lead to the
colonization of the lifeworld.

Finally, Habermas highlights the importance of
Mead's social behaviourism in the construction, as we
also saw above. Indeed, it enabled him to show the sense
in which psychological individuation is an effect of the
internalization of the symbolically mediated communicative process.[61] And, above all, it could be combined or
made compatible or *convergent* with the Piagetian and
Kohlbergian programme of developmental psychology,
a necessary reference in the overall construction for all
of the reasons outlined above.

3. Once the basic claims of the theory of communicative action have been laid out and justified, Habermas
can defend the originality and theoretical force of
reconstructive epistemology.This is the aim of the following two articles, the first indirectly and the second
directly.[62] The first does in fact make the connection
with the critical themes, but this time taking the reference to Weber as its starting point. Indeed, Weber was
the first modern sociologist to conceive of a kind of
dialectic of modernity starting from rationalization and
the extension of instrumental rationality to become an
'iron cage' – a central theme of Weberian Marxism from
Lukács to Marcuse via Horkheimer and Adorno. As we
have seen, Habermas reformulated this line of theory in
functionalist terms but also in terms of the twin concepts
of instrumental rationality and communicative rationality, which enabled him to correct the pessimism of the
first generation of critical theorists by demonstrating the
difference between and complementarity of instrumental
and communicative rationalization. The second article
underlines the novelty of the reconstructive model by

comparison with that of understanding and thus also how it can provide an epistemologically innovative response to the critical challenge posed by Weber in the previous article. As we have seen, Chomsky's generative theory transposed to the rules of verbal communication made it possible at an epistemological level to retain both a dimension of understanding necessary for grasping the symbolic dimension of social action (as in Gadamer) and also a fallibilistic dimension (as in Popper and against Gadamer), because the social agent must follow rules that can be reconstructed by the theorist. But the theme of reconstruction must also be related to the detranscendentalization of reason, which Habermas now considers to be *incorporated* into everyday practice and therefore to be an object of *explanation* or *reconstruction* rather than of a theory in the strict sense. Rationality exists in reality and in a substantial and varied way.[63]

4. In conclusion, Habermas spells out the overall physiognomy of modern society as depicted by the theory of communicative action.[64] Here the diagnosis of a dialectic of reason – inaugurated by Kant, plunged into history by Hegel, and modified first by Marx, then by Weber and finally by Adorno and Horkheimer – achieves a kind of fulfilment. But it is a fulfilment corrected by the twin concepts of instrumental and communicative action, which enables Habermas to develop a conception of modernity as dialectical differentiation and rationalization, according to the picture evoked above in the first part. As a result, he is able to grasp the differentiated dimension of the normative core of modernity, while at the same time providing a more balanced account of the pathologies of modernity than that of the excessively homogenizing critiques of modernity in Western Marxism from Lukács to Adorno, in Heidegger or in postmodernist interpretations of modernity. Thus, Habermas produced a theory capable of accounting for the historical material of the study on the

structural transformations of the public sphere, while in the background revising the ambivalent relationship to democratic modernity of large parts of German thought since Romanticism and German idealism.

B. Rationality, truth and justification

Habermas initially approached the questions of language, rationality and knowledge from the angle of the coordination of action and reasoned discussion, central themes of his reconstruction of historical materialism informed by the dialectic of the public sphere, having abandoned the theory of knowledge of *Knowledge and Human Interests*, as we have seen. What is involved, therefore, is an *internal clarification* that also faces the challenge of *readjusting* retrospectively the construction of the 1970s. Therefore, Habermas re-examines the claim to truth and revises the theory of meaning he initially forged in the early 1970s, drawing upon the criticisms of the correspondence theory of truth. In particular, he discusses the readjustment of the consensual theory of truth to which he was constrained by Rorty's contextualism, even though he had initially regarded the rationalist position he defended in the 1980s to be *sufficient* in his debate against postmodernism.[65] As a result, Habermas encounters the problem of realism at the heart of the analytical philosophy of language since Quine and revises his theory of rationality in part in a realistic direction. This revision also points indirectly to his mode of theoretical construction by convergences and overlaps discussed above, which initially inspired the notion of a kind of symmetry between the different claims to validity.

Habermas presents the material in four stages. First, he addresses the linguistic turn in which he situates himself from a historical perspective. Then, in the second and third stages, he elucidates his theory of rationality centred on formal pragmatism and his theory of truth, in both cases integrating the realist readjustment and its implications. Finally, again by way of conclusion, he discusses the destiny of realism in the theory of knowledge following the linguistic turn. I will address these aspects in turn.[66]

1. Habermas's first task is to situate his theory of meaning and of formal pragmatics within the history of the philosophy of language and within the development of his own theory. Reason progressively appears as historically situated and connected with language and action. Thus, Habermas must show how his theory of communication fits into and adjusts to this history, exhibiting what it owes to the different figures whose names mark this process of *detranscendentalization*.

As we have seen, Apel was the first to draw his attention to the convergences between the tradition claimed by Gadamer, extending from Humboldt to Heidegger, and the analytical tradition, which from Frege to Wittgenstein also underwent a protracted development towards understanding. But, even though these two traditions in part achieve detranscendentalization by inscribing language into history and society respectively, they are nevertheless vulnerable to the criticism that they retain an *excessively transcendental* conception of understanding, immunized against the forms of *learning* imposed by the confrontation with the natural world and the human world. The theories of understanding and meaning must therefore be embedded within a *broader* understanding of the functions of linguistic exchange in communication and discourse, with rational acceptability having a *normative* dimension that may necessitate a *revision* of our linguistic relation to the world.[67]

This is why Habermas has to develop a sufficiently *complete* theory of meaning.[68] As in the case of the theory of communicative action and the competing theories of action, this is a matter of demonstrating the integrative power of formal pragmatics compared to competing – and specifically also excessively one-sided – theories of meaning. Habermas mentions three such theories: intentionalist semantics, which focuses on the speaker's intention; formal semantics, whose object is the truth of the propositions; and the semantics of the use of meanings in contexts of interaction. However, the different claims to validity refer to the different functions of language in communication and hence to the *interconnected unity* of these three aspects: saying something to someone about something.[69] This is what enables us to grasp the normative import of speech acts. Here again, one of the philosophical advantages of Habermas's theory is its integrative character.

2. Next, it must be shown how Habermas can integrate the realist readjustment he undertook in the 1990s into this movement of detranscendentalization which nevertheless leaves an important place for the normativity of reason. In order to grasp fully the meaning of these developments, we must go back and discuss more directly the content of the article to which Habermas refers.[70] Since reviving the Hegelian theme of the opposition between work and interaction, Habermas had made a contrast between two types of action (namely, instrumental and strategic action oriented to success, on the one hand, and communicative action oriented to agreement, on the other), and thus between two forms of rationality situated on the same level, as it were, which served as a guiding thread in his evolutionary theory.

The guiding principle here, therefore, is in the first instance a revival of the question of the place of communicative rationality in relation to rationality in general, given that there cannot be any question of reducing rationality as a whole to argumentative rationality.[71] Thus, Habermas distinguishes three distinct and intertwined roots of rationality: the propositional structure of knowledge, the teleological structure of action and the communicative structure of discourse. They are distinct because none of them can serve as the exclusive basis for the other two, and they are intertwined because each of them presupposes a relationship with language and action: epistemic rationality as the medium of knowledge, of its confrontation with reality and its possible revision; teleological rationality as the appropriate calculation of means; and communicative rationality to establish agreement. Now it is precisely this common relationship to language and action that is taken up by the practice of justification. In this respect, the practice of justification does not play a *foundational* role but merely occupies a *transversal* position, because in discussion the practice of justification connects a propositional element that must be justified, a teleological element – because it is a matter of restoring coordination – and a communicative element – because it is a discussion with others about something. Thus, discussion or the practice of justification occurs when epistemic knowledge, the seriousness or relevance of actions, or agreement are challenged or become problematic.

Presenting discourse as this transversal space common to the different roots of rationality calls for a partial revision of the theory of understanding, because neither in the case of knowledge nor in that of action does language mobilize the 'you' in affirmative or intentional propositions, but only the 'I' and the 'he/she/it'. Thus, one can in effect conceive of two types of agreement: agreement in the strong sense, when the 'you' is summoned in such a way that the reasons supporting the validity of the speech act are recognized and shared by specific appeal to a shared lifeworld; and agreement in the weak sense, when the reasons supporting the speech act are *only recognized* without being shared, and thus are nevertheless valid or rational *from the point of view of the actor or the speaker* who behaves monologically in representing the world or planning an action. For a long time, Habermas thought that overtly strategic uses of language, such as threats or insults, represent derivative and parasitic cases of action oriented to agreement, and thus he accorded the latter original status. Against this first thesis, however, which Apel criticized in 1994,[72] Habermas could now object that understanding a speech act (the key issue since the Gauss Lectures) is a matter of knowing the conditions of the illocutionary or *perlocutionary* success that a speaker can achieve thanks to this act. This presupposes the ability to recognize as valid both reasons that are independent of the actor and *actor-relative* reasons, so that agreement and cooperation can be conceived in either a strong or a weak sense.[73]

The long following article discussed by Habermas has the complementary objective of resituating communicative reason within the historical and intellectual movement of detranscendentalization by thematizing the counterfactual presuppositions underlying the normativity of the claims to validity that inform the various speech acts.[74] It does so by taking Kant and his normative stance, in contrast to that of Humean empiricism, as its point of reference. This also involves a critical confrontation with the analytic tradition (Frege, Davidson, Dummett and Brandom) on this twofold terrain of the normativity of reason in a detranscendentalized context. The comparison with Kant enables Habermas to show that the Kantian dualisms (transcendental/empirical, noumenon/phenomenon, constitutive/regulative, transcendental/immanent, etc.), which still have strong metaphysical connotations and are inscribed in the mentalist paradigm – hence predate the linguistic turn and its complementary pragmatic and hermeneutical dimensions – are *translated* into a *detranscendentalized* and weak form in communicative reason. The language game of agreement presupposes only rules connected with idealizing presuppositions, such as the existence of a shared world of independent objects, and that it is possible for participants to support context-transcending claims to validity in a responsible manner. Thus, after the realist turn, the opposition between reality in itself and phenomena can be said to be translated into the opposition between truth and rational acceptability, as we shall see in what follows regarding the realist reconfiguration of the theory of truth. In discourse properly speaking, these counterfactual presuppositions are expanded and made explicit in the form of the requirements of publicity, inclusion, equality and sincerity, without which the reasons exchanged cannot inspire conviction. This does not ensure that the debates are indeed such, but only that the participants would not engage in the discussion if they were not able to think of these rules as being operative. Thus, the critical confrontation with the representatives of the analytical tradition enables Habermas to show that the normative dimension of meaning presupposes agreement with its idealizing presuppositions.

3. This linkage of reason and meaning can then be approached from the angle of the theory of truth before and after the realist turn, respectively. This is the subject of the following two articles discussed by Habermas. The first,[75] which is contemporary with the Gauss Lectures, turns on the critique of the correspondence theory of truth and the theory of validity constructed by Habermas by generalizing the case of assertoric propositions. Truth is then conceived as the claim raised by a constative speech act, a claim in need of support by reasons that can be exchanged in a discussion regulated by the counterfactual idealizations mentioned above. It cannot be understood in the first instance as correspondence or evidence. The following article,[76] which was written over twenty-five years later in response

to Rorty's sceptical stance, corrects this position by showing, contrary to the author of *Philosophy and the Mirror of Nature*, that truth cannot be reduced to its guarantee by justification.

The project of constructing a social theory embedded in a theory of agreement grounded in formal pragmatics inclined Habermas to defend a discursive conception of validity in general and of truth in particular – that is, to make an audacious and unfounded *generalization* of the *special case* of the validity of *norms* and moral judgements into a conception of validity *reduced to rational acceptability*, relying initially on Toulmin and later also on Dummett. Thus, from the article on theories of truth onwards (which is therefore the first of the two articles selected), Habermas interpreted truth in consensual terms founded on the difference between, on the one hand, the subject–representation–object relation corresponding to the practical context of the action and referring to objective or subjective information, and, on the other, the simultaneously vertical and horizontal relation anchored in the context of argumentation – namely, the vertical relation between linguistic proposition (or utterance) and state of affairs and the horizontal relation between a speaker and a hearer established by the claim to validity of this proposition. In this way, Habermas constructed a consensual or discursive theory of truth by anchoring it explicitly in the project of constructing a social theory and of grounding moral theory.[77] In this respect, the idea of a truth as correspondence was both reserved for the context of instrumental action and referred in the context of argumentation to a particular type of reasons (perceptual experiences of the participants in the discussion) which, being subjective, must be validated in the linguistic forms of exchange *whose telos is agreement* in order to be considered valid justifications of a theoretical or cognitive utterance. Thus, Habermas insisted on the distance and reflexivity implied by the notion of truth, while also insisting that the claim to validity of correctness *shared these characteristics*, unlike these two other claims to validity, namely intelligibility and sincerity.

The power and the reception of Rorty's contextualist position, combined with the general debate on postmodernism and the more specific debate on realism, compelled Habermas to rethink this difference, and therefore indirectly to reinstate a difference between the claims to validity of rightness and truth. He did so by connecting the claim to truth with the Piagetian concept of learning, complementing it with a theory of reference borrowed from Putnam, and by according greater importance to Peirce.[78] The principle informing this realist correction is easy to understand: if the relativization of the realist core of the idea of truth as correspondence rested on the clear difference between the contexts of action and discourse, the reintroduction of this realist core calls for a pragmatist reintroduction of the context of action *into* the context of discourse. This explains the frequently asserted strategic character of the co-originality of action, representation and communication. It is thus a matter of giving the discursive relation between truth and justification a pragmatic inflection in order to reintroduce something which had escaped it. Moreover, this has to be done by linking the point of view of the observer, for whom, following the linguistic, hermeneutic and pragmatic turns, we can no longer credibly claim that they have access to the naked facts, *and* the participant's point of view with the associated everyday realist intuitions. As a product of adaptation, learning has a naturalistic and objectivist meaning; but it also has a *lived* meaning that is confirmed from the first-person perspective as *progress*. The subject of knowledge can compare two cognitions of an object *for him-* or *herself* by relying both on the pragmatic presupposition of a world external to our representations that exists in an identical way for first, second and third persons, and on the discrete indexical properties of each of these two descriptions of the same thing, neither of which can exhaust the description of the independent reality to which they refer. Thus, the two descriptions refer to a reality *internal* to our practices and they can be compared in discourse, *but* with the aim of establishing which of them is *the most reliable* for our practice and our confrontation with reality, where discourse represents a *fallibilistic virtualization* of our practices.

4. Thus, in conclusion, Habermas's aim is to underline the specific form that realism assumes after the linguistic turn or in the wider context of detranscendentalized thought: it is necessarily an *internal* form of realism that does not presuppose an absolute point of view.[79]

C. *Ethics, morality and communicative competence*

The development of discourse ethics must first be situated in relation to three determinants taken together: the reaction to substantialism, the influence of Apel and the construction of social theory.

In fact, the intellectual background of discourse ethics is the rejection of the conservative moral philosophy inspired by Aristotle and by the Right Hegelianism of Joachim Ritter and his circle, which, as we saw above, represented a kind of euphemized and ambiguous continuity with the Nazi period. On the other hand, Apel had developed his ethical theory in the early 1970s based on a conception of the communication community that reinterprets Kant in Peircean terms and in critical opposition to positivism and decisionism concerning values.[80] Habermas was in a position to develop his own reconstructive and interdisciplinary version of discourse ethics connected with social theory from 1971 to 1972 onwards when he constructed a theory of the development of personality structures oriented to linguistic coordination and justification practices that took the form of a theory of the stages of development of interactive competence.[81] But he did not actually *spell out* and *develop* this aspect of his thought until the early 1980s, that is, until he had completed the communicative reformulation of the programme of first-generation Critical Theory. Moreover, he did so in an international context that had been rejuvenated in particular by Rawls's *Theory of Justice* and the new agenda of the reactions it prompted, especially among communitarians (MacIntyre, Taylor and Walzer).

The starting point is quite simple: norms of interaction are elucidated in discourse, which shows that, from the performative perspective of practical agents and participants in discourse, we expect that actions will be justified with reasons. In the case of claims to rightness, for example, it is a matter of justifying the reasons for warnings, orders or recommendations. It is clear that the rules governing discourse with their counterfactual presuppositions (inclusion, equality, sincerity, etc.) function as a selective test of acceptable reasons. Therefore, it must be possible to reconstruct, in the epistemological sense we encountered above, the deontological dimension of practical discourse, which can serve as a basis for a discursive moral theory and provide a postmetaphysical variant of the categorical imperative. This is what Habermas would do with his two principles (U) and (D).

The principle (U) is a rule of universalization that *spells out* the *pragmatic presuppositions* of practical discourse that are brought to bear by practical agents who have reached the postconventional level of motivational development (the level normally generalized in post-traditional societies) when they are faced with a practical conflict. They must consider that, in order to be valid, a norm must satisfy the condition that the consequences and side effects which can be expected to result from its *universal* observation for the satisfaction of the interests of each individual can be freely accepted by *all* persons concerned. The principle (D) seeks to defend the proceduralism of discourse ethics on a more directly philosophical level: 'Only those norms can claim to be valid that meet (or could meet) with the approval of all affected in their capacity as participants in a practical discourse.'[82] It expresses the procedural idea that the validity of norms is conditioned exclusively by the participation in practical discourses of those affected by its application. Thus, it prohibits at the philosophical level the idea of a determined *philosophical production* of valid norms, which differentiates it both from philosophical substantialism (whether neo-Aristotelian or neo-Hegelian) and from a highly determined theory of justice such as that of Rawls with all of its concrete prescriptions. Thus, its radically procedural character reinforces the cognitivism, universalism and formalism of (U): it draws our attention to the fact that (U) expresses only the normative content of a will formed through discourse. In this sense, the position defended by Habermas is more radically procedural than other competing deontological ethical theories. It should also be noted that the relationship between (U) and (D) is a 'vertical' and complementary one: on the one hand, (D) presupposes that the choice of norms is open to justification (i.e., that a social situation exists in which subjects possess the necessary competences to perform the intellectual work of justification) and, on the other hand, (D) grounds the selectivity of (U) with regard to evaluative or ethical choices in the narrow sense.

The highly reflexive and abstract character of (D) and (U) is also incompatible with the idea of a world of hypostatized moral norms which would have an analogous status to that of the facts in the epistemic language game (or in simple descriptions) and in the language game of theoretical discussion. Habermas ultimately reintroduced the latter form of realism into his treatment of theoretical discourse, having previously excluded it in the article on theories of truth, precisely because he was misled by an excessive concern for symmetry into conceiving of theoretical discourse on the model of practical discourse.[83] Contrary to what some Platonist positions of Kohlberg's might suggest, there is no such thing as moral 'knowledge'[84] comparable in structure to cognitive knowledge.

Here, therefore, Habermas chose to address two dimensions of his theory in turn, through two groups of articles. The articles in the first group spell out the principles of discourse ethics, connect it with the theory of communicative action and situate it within the sequence of positions in moral philosophy; the articles in the second group deal with the overall architecture of practical reason and the readjustments to the theory of law and the theory of reference. I will address these aspects in turn.[85]

1. Having reviewed the intellectual sources and the principles of discourse ethics (as we have just done),[86] Habermas underlines the respects in which it is better able than Kant's moral theory to deal with the Hegelian objections of formalism, abstraction, the impotence of the 'ought' and the terrorism of pure conviction, these being the objections brought against Rawls by communitarians like Charles Taylor.[87] In particular, he demonstrates its roots in the theory of socialization and a theory of society, and thus also in a theory of *ethical life*, while presenting this theory of moral life as a theory of reciprocal recognition with its *idealistic presuppositions* and not just a theory of *ties* and evaluative *sources* as with the communitarians.[88] Habermas is also able to explain that discourse ethics does *not* represent a normative philosophical reorientation following Critical Theory, but instead an elucidation and local clarification of his theory from the point of view of the participants in practical discourse.[89]

Then, in the final two articles in this first group, Habermas situates discourse ethics within the space of contemporary moral positions opened up by Rawls and the reactions to his work and within European history.[90] For Habermas, Rawls's evolution towards a political conception of justice concedes too much to the neo-Aristotelianism of the communitarians, and thus to a strong conception of the good and even to religion, by weakening Kantian constructivism in response to their objections. Habermas's deontological theory does not have to do this, as we just saw in the case of his theory of ethical life and as will become clear below concerning religion. A universalist morality, therefore, is not necessarily homogenizing. On the contrary, if it is *sufficiently differentiated*, it shows the real possibility of *inclusion* in a discussion whose idealizing presuppositions must make it possible to reach a consensus between *different worldviews* by urging them to engage in forms of *decentring* and thus of *learning*.

2. Thus, Habermas can outline the overall physiognomy of practical reason and then examine the meaning of the realist turn for his moral position.

He distinguishes three uses of reason – pragmatic, ethical and moral – each of which refers to different practical situations.[91] The pragmatic use concerns rational action directed to an end; it presupposes that the relevant values and norms are already fixed and it is governed by hypothetical imperatives of prudence and skill. The ethical use concerns an individual's choices of basic values which he or she must embody in order to enjoy a good and happy life; it presupposes a hermeneutical understanding of oneself and the traditions to which one adheres and it is expressed especially in one's life choices. These two uses of practical reason, corresponding respectively to utilitarianism and Aristotle (and Gadamer), remain largely self-centred. By contrast, the strictly 'moral' use presupposes in the first place the decentring of the first-person point of view because it comes into play in normative conflicts. It was Kant who identified the moral use of practical reason, but in a postmetaphysical form.

But we must dissipate the potential confusion of moral cognitivism with moral realism, especially following the realist turn in the theory of reference discussed above. This requires us to *break with a certain notion of symmetry* between the different claims to validity and show that there is no such thing as a world of moral facts comparable to the world of facts that would enable us to conceive an equivalent in the moral domain of the difference between truth and justification.[92] The purpose of practical, in contrast to theoretical, discourse is not to ensure practical certainty in the moral world, but to produce a consensus. From this point of view the interplay between the decentring of perspectives and counterfactual presuppositions is *sufficient* to ensure the validity of the norms resulting from the discursive process.

The final article selected and discussed by Habermas[93] makes a connection with the following introduction on law by showing how, within the frame of reference of the theory of communicative action, morality and law both *overlap* and are *distinct*, and thus have to *complement* each other *increasingly* on an evolutionary scale, in each case from the dual point of view of the observer and the participant.[94] This invites Habermas to make a kind of redeployment of the principle of discourse. It is no longer tied exclusively to 'discourse ethics' but is understood instead, in a more general sense, as a simple procedure for the impartial foundation of norms of action that can be specified differently in ethical-moral as opposed to legal discourses, where the latter draw on a *broader spectrum of reasons*. In this way, he can underline the differences from Apel, who for Habermas remains much too close to the Kantian idea of a metaphysics of morals produced by the philosopher. Like Rawls's position, this position remains metaphysically too strong.

D. *Procedure, rule of law and learning*

In the fourth introduction, Habermas discusses a number of central historical and biographical factors that offer insight not only into his political philosophy, but also, as we saw above, into his choices in related philosophical fields (such as postmetaphysical thinking). His opposition to the sacrificial and substantialist voluntarism and decisionism of National Socialism and its pre- and post-war scholarly versions in Carl Schmitt, coupled with his opposition to Arnold Gehlen's conservative anthropology and to Niklas Luhmann's systems theory, lend more than merely a contrastive meaning to the understanding of democracy as inclusion and deliberation, but also to discursive rationality and to the theory of society and, more generally, to the rejection of elitism and philosophical esotericism. It should be added that the theory of law is also a response to Rawls's theory of justice. Habermas defends a theory that is both more sociological and more procedural because it argues that the theorist *cannot* proceed on the basis of a *fixed repertoire* of reasons and therefore of a 'theory of justice' in Rawls's sense, as we have just seen in the case of Habermas's version of discourse ethics.

At the same time, the theory of law involves an important *theoretical and diagnostic readjustment* with regard to law and its function by comparison with the *Theory of Communicative Action*. There, inspired by Weber and Luhmann, Habermas viewed law as at least in part a kind of extension of power (G) that colonizes the communicatively structured lifeworld (I), even though he contrasted with this perspective the normative force of communicative action as embodied in the basic rights enshrined in the constitution. Habermas is now more concerned to grasp its *role as an interface* between I (and L) and G and A, in its totality and structure. It is a matter of readjusting the unstable part of the diagnosis of the colonization of the lifeworld by law formulated in the *Theory of Communicative Action*, while addressing the question of global social integration in general alongside systemic integration (by money and power as codified media, A and G) and social integration (or communicative integration, I and L). Law seems to be an intermediate category, linked on the one side to the systems of administrative power and the market and on the other side to the lived norm, so that it enables functional integration in general (AGIL).

Between Facts and Norms is a typical Habermasian postmetaphysical construct: it combines the epistemology of frames of reference with its systematized evolutionary stages, reconstructive epistemology, and the hermeneutic and constructive epistemology of justification by stages of the choice of theoretical materials in a process that proceeds from the abstract to the concrete. The two series of constraints (on the one hand, the normative constraints of discourse theory and, on the other, the functional constraints) enable him to reconstruct the architecture of the modern rule of law with its hierarchy of norms, its institutions and its connection with the political sovereignty that emanates from discussions in the public sphere, and all of this in an ideal-typical way at the postconventional stage of the evolutionary dynamic. As with the *Theory of Communicative Action* discussed in the first introduction and the first collection of articles, the format prevents Habermas from presenting the constructive justification procedure of the whole theory of law developed in *Between Facts and Norms*. In contrast to the second, third and fifth introductions, therefore, here we have an outline of principles instead of a genuinely complete presentation.

If we follow Habermas's introduction (and the

four groups of articles he presents), then it is a question both of defending in a progressive movement of enlargement the procedural model of reason in the modern political field – that is, of demonstrating its explanatory power for understanding the modern rule of law and its structure – and of inscribing the discursive procedure in the whole evolution of modern society and international institutions. I will address these four themes in turn.[95]

1. The first task is to demonstrate the epistemic force of the procedural and reconstructive model of democracy. The procedure in question refers to legitimation through the citizens' participation in deliberative discussion. This is the topic of the first three articles selected and introduced by Habermas.

The first article,[96] written to mark the bicentenary of the French Revolution, seems to have played an initiating role in the construction of the theory of law following the Tanner Lectures on 'Law and Morality',[97] which were already moving in this direction. It seeks to highlight the propulsive historical force of this moment when the notion of citizenship defined by participation and deliberation was put into practice. Furthermore, it details the modern antagonisms that break out in favour of this revolution, in particular between the proponents of the social republic inspired by Rousseau and those of human rights inspired by liberal thinkers such as Locke, an opposition which was taken up and deepened by being connected with the economy of the antagonism between socialism and liberalism. These intellectual and historical antagonisms can be explained and overcome if we consider that the sovereign people must not be conceived as an entity, but instead in terms of the decentralized and desubstantialized process of informal discussions presupposing the rights of citizens as understood by the liberal tradition, where the discussions in question can programme the agenda of relevant topics and reasons for an administrative political apparatus that otherwise always tends to become self-enclosed in a bureaucratic manner.[98]

Habermas could then develop this intuition in an ideal-typical fashion at the level of political theory by spelling out the difference between the liberal and republican models of democracy and explaining how the same dialectics – the oppositions between freedom and equality, between pluralism and unity, between civil rights and participation rights, etc. – are resolved by the model of deliberative democracy.[99]

The third article, which Habermas discusses quite briefly, illustrates what we said earlier about *reconstruction* and the role played by *complementary hypotheses*.[100] Once the theoretical core of the practice and the model of law has been reconstructed thanks to the two interwoven series of normative and functional constraints, a whole series of hypotheses can be *added* to describe a reality rich in normative and factual determinations. These may include empirical and critical hypotheses about unfavourable conditions of socialization or, after the realist turn, about the secondary role of agreement in the weak sense (compromise, negotiations). By comparison with *Between Facts and Norms*, therefore, this represents a *more concrete* segment of construction in the Hegelian or Marxist sense. This affords Habermas an opportunity to demonstrate the descriptive superiority of his model, which combines elements of sociology, political theory and jurisprudence, over the models belonging exclusively to one of these disciplines, by showing how the agenda of themes and the repertoire of reasons constituting public opinion is produced in the public sphere in discourses and informal arenas, in the media system and, finally, the institutional political arena, thanks to the different types of social actors (citizens, associations, political parties, trade unions, etc.). As in the case of the theories of social action and of meaning, the salient philosophical advantage of the theory of law is its integrative power.

2. This superiority of the interdisciplinary approach of discourse theory is demonstrated once again by the connection to Habermas's theory as a whole and to the enlarged perspective of the evolutionary dynamic.[101] Habermas elucidates the connections between the constitutional state (the rule of law, the division of powers and respect for civil liberties) and democracy (self-determination and popular sovereignty) by showing how the dynamics of the dissolution of the sacred or cosmic order means that legality can henceforth be legitimized only by the combined means of public and private autonomy, by popular sovereignty and human rights, because self-determination presupposes that citizens develop their opinions freely. It is the ideal-typical framework of evolutionary logic that enables Habermas to show how, in a *postconventional*, differentiated and rationalized society, citizens, who are simultaneously members of civil society, must determine their common destiny by recognizing each other's civil rights without which collective deliberation lacks the ability to legitimize and motivate. The strong forms of sacred or metaphysical authority have lost their motivational power as a result of the increasing devaluation of the *conventional* (cosmological, traditional) type of reasons that these forms of authority are able to mobilize.[102]

3. Having resituated his theory of law within the broad outlines of evolutionary theory, Habermas can address the shifting terrain of historical dynamics. The third series of articles deals with the theory of social differentiation and learning where these are connected, as we saw in the first part, with a theory of *occasional causes leading to a progressive or regressive development* in the motivational structure of interactive competence, and thus potentially also in institutions and culture. Here Habermas applies this scheme to the place

of national culture and religion in their specific relation to modern politics, in particular in their respective roles as resources for argumentation. Solidarity, which is mediated by verbal communication, is thus susceptible of transformation in this medium. Here, then, we touch on the very abundant material of Habermas's political writings.

First Habermas evokes how European history has provoked waves of differentiation predicated on learning processes involving an interplay between *ethnos* and *demos*. Nationalism and its ravages, the development of weaponry that makes a mockery of the idea of a noble death for one's fatherland and postcolonial consciousness have operated as *occasional causes*, provoking either pathological regressions at the level of identities or, on the contrary, a learning process capable of decoupling the still conventional dimension of the identity of the people from its counterfactually inclusive postconventional dimension of self-determination – hence which is capable of differentiating between *ethnos* and *demos*.[103] But these learning and differentiation processes, which, as in the case of morality, refer to the subordination of conventional to postconventional motivations, must not be confused either with the postmodernist critique of the identity and universality of the law or with a strong multiculturalist position.[104] Nevertheless, we must *also* raise the question of the symbolic price of the learning process, especially for religion, which is forced to fit into the mould of this new division of normative labour of postconventional society, as we shall see below.[105]

4. The final section of the text discusses the extension of the procedural theory of law to international law in accordance with the same principles.[106] The paths laid out by Kant for the project of perpetual peace are both resumed and criticized in the light of the new series of *occasional causes* contributed by history and of a

detranscendentalized conception of inclusive learning institutionalized in the medium of law. He argues that the totalitarian wars and the Nuremberg trials, the collapse of the Berlin Wall and the militarized export of human rights during the first and second Gulf Wars – justified by American neo-conservatives by appeal to Hobbes, Strauss and Schmitt – should spur a transnational institutionalization of the communicative process in which private and public autonomy, hence the two corresponding dimensions of human rights, are interwoven. The outline of a global society based on both the national sovereignty of the states and the human rights of world citizens can inspire a partial reorganization of international institutions.

E. Detranscendentalization, critique and transcendence
Here, Habermas addresses three apparently distinct topics: the framework of detranscendentalization and its implications for philosophical methodology and the conception of reason, the question of naturalism, and the question of religion. The first and third points are developed in two stages.

However, it is a matter of the same thing unfolding its consequences, starting from the framework of detranscendentalization and its link back to the social theory of differentiation and rationalization, a framework and correspondence that were first spelled out in the 1980s in the context of the debate on postmodernism, later of the spectacular rise of the neurosciences and, finally, of the debate on the 'return of religion'.

I will take my lead from Habermas in discussing these three aspects in turn.[107]

1. As we have seen, the question of normalization and his suspicion concerning a strong conception of philosophy stemming from German idealism intersected, for Habermas, with the influences of Löwith and Apel and the aspiration to reconstruct historical materialism

as a critical theory. These perspectives combined to lend a certain esoteric and prophetic, stylized and aristocratic strain within German philosophy, invented by the Romantics and the German idealists and ultimately embodied in an ideal-typical manner by Heidegger, the appearance of a reactive and metaphysical, idealist survival in Marx's sense, whereas the Left-Hegelian generation seemed to represent a vanguard of detranscendentalization and postmetaphysical thinking.[108] Moreover, the intellectual reconstruction of detranscendentalization as a sequence of stages with its paradigms and turns and its relation of correspondence back to the social theory of differentiation and rationalization can be understood as a kind of enriched and more complex continuation of Marx's critique of ideology.

Within the intellectual space defined by these coordinates, the constructive exercise of philosophy renounces both privileged means and excessive architectonic ambitions, such as that of assigning their place to the various scientific disciplines that have become almost independent of philosophy since the nineteenth century.[109] Postmetaphysical thinking must be situated within the coordinates of the sequencing of paradigms and turns, at the modest endpoint of a fallible mode of thinking that relies on collaboration with the results of other disciplines and understands reason as tied to history, language and action. Thus, the philosopher does not try to illuminate universal history in a prophetic manner (like Heidegger) or even to propose its radical transformation (like Marx) but integrates him- or herself in a fallibilist and realist spirit into a differentiated world constituted by spheres of value that are largely independent of philosophy. At the point of intersection of these spheres, the primary role of the philosopher is to translate the languages into each other, provided that he or she is also informed about what these languages involve thanks to other intellectual disciplines. The intellectual who intervenes in public debates cannot rely on anything except the strength and precision of his or her arguments, and must renounce all other forms of authority and narcissism. Here again it becomes apparent what constitutes, at least in part, the implicit protagonist of this deflationary revision of philosophy, namely a certain strain of German philosophy with grandiose but inordinate aspirations, that of German Romanticism and idealism, which seeks the secret keys to universal history and cultivates an aloof and esoteric attitude.

Moreover, the unity of a detranscendentalized conception of reason (i.e. one understood in post-ontological, postmentalist, linguistic, hermeneutic and pragmatic terms) but one which is also communicative (i.e., intersubjective and not logocentric) and is adjusted to the modern movement of differentiation and rationalization of social action, is henceforth essentially a procedural unity.[110] It is based exclusively on the rules governing argumentation and in particular on the counterfactual idealizing power that these rules presuppose among the participants in argumentation.[111]

2. and 3. The two following aspects are presented as a kind of postmetaphysical antinomy that opposes the hard variants of natural science, on the one hand, and religion, on the other, the former reinforced by discoveries in genetics, the latter by the 'return of religion'. This is reminiscent of the two major currents opposed by Critical Theory in the 1930s: the Vienna Circle and ontologism. From this point of view, Horkheimer's project of a critique of reason based on the interdisciplinary materialism of postmetaphysical thinking does indeed find a continuation in Habermas's theory in a more systematic, constructive form, for all the reasons that we saw at the outset, and in a partially transformed context.

Thus, Habermas begins by addressing the question of naturalism in its hard variants. Taking his inspiration from Husserl – specifically, the notion of the *Lebenswelt* from *Ideen* and that of an objectivist self-understanding of science from *Krisis*[112] – Habermas shows, within his own sociological framework of differentiation and detranscendentalization, that scientistic naturalism reflects a reductionist self-understanding of science that both forgets its anchoring in the lifeworld and overestimates its own intellectual powers of generalization. Science can no longer produce a true image of the world. Thus, the new scientism of neural materialism reduces the plurality of the differentiated (epistemic, normative and expressive) aspects of the lifeworld to the single dimension of objectivity, but also to causal mechanisms. However, the symbolic and rule-governed dimension of interactions presupposes the first-person point of view of social agents, who regard themselves performatively as answerable to each other for their discursive commitments, and who therefore cannot and must not adopt the exclusive, third-person singular observer point of view on their language game.[113]

With regard to religion, Habermas addresses the efforts at self-transformation that the major religions have had to undertake in order to become compatible with a rationalized and differentiated modernity, in which science, politics, morality and art have emancipated themselves from religious tutelage, which calls for both a renunciation of all forms of authoritarian and political imposition of religion and a highly reflexive and hermeneutic relationship to its own core of revealed faith.[114] But this same process also assigns to religion the role of a resource of meaning and motivation that is useful or even irreplaceable for this same modern society, whose historical dynamics tend to dry up sources of motivation.[115] Religion is useful or even irreplaceable in effect because, in a society that is pluralistic and liberal, and must therefore be neutral towards worldviews, it has preserved a relationship with the images of the world and the strong perspectives of salvation that tend to be lacking in a secularized society. This presupposes that the language of postmetaphysical thinking and the language of religion can be translated into one another in a reflexive and hermeneutic way.[116] In this case, therefore, it is the paths laid out by Kant in *Religion within the Boundaries of Mere Reason* that Habermas re-translates into the detranscendentalized and intersubjectivist coordinates of his social theory and the theory of postmetaphysical reason with the aim of promoting a dialogue between postmetaphysical philosophy and reflective religion within the public sphere of democratic societies.

We are now in a position to depict the tree of Habermas's theory even in its more technical ramifications: the roots (detranscendentalization), its trunk comprising his social theory, its main branches represented by his theory of reason, his moral theory and his theory of law and, finally, the secondary branches constituted by the relations between modern reason and science, on the one hand, and religion, on the other. In this way, these five retrospective introductory texts on his contribution to philosophy can be situated within the immense construction project of the Habermasian oeuvre.

1

Foundations of Sociology in the Theory of Language

The Christian Gauss Lectures, which I delivered at Princeton University in 1971, mark a visible caesura in my philosophical development.[1] To be sure, my preoccupation with issues in the philosophy of language can be traced back to my student days – among other things, to a seminar with Erich Rothacker and Leo Weisgerber on Wilhelm von Humboldt's theory of language. The most important formative influence was provided by discussions with my friend and mentor Karl-Otto Apel,[2] which had prepared me for the encounter with Wittgenstein's *Philosophical Investigations* and Gadamer's *Truth and Method*[3] and later inspired me to read Charles Sanders Peirce's theory of language and semiotics. Thus, I had already begun to make a *linguistic turn* in the review essay *On the Logic of the Social Sciences* (1967)[4] and shortly afterwards in my communicative interpretation of the structural model of psychoanalysis in *Knowledge and Human Interests* (1968).[5] But my sociological investigations (1962)[6] and my reflections on social philosophy (1963)[7] remained within the ambit of the Frankfurt tradition until the late 1960s.

Until then, I had not questioned the theoretical background of the older critical theory as such, even though I had been suspicious from the beginning of its implicit thinking in terms of the philosophy of history and of Adorno's 'covert orthodoxy' (specifically, his tacit acceptance of Marx's theory of surplus value). Since my dissertation, I had been tormented by the question of how to reconcile a radical form of historical thinking with the justification of a substantive normative diagnosis of the present. The more familiar I became with empirical studies of contemporary societies, the less the horizontal differentiation and accelerated increase in complexity of contemporary social life seemed to be compatible with the holism of the Hegelian-Marxist paradigm.[8] The same reasons reinforced my doubts about the conceptual foundations of the idealist tradition in the philosophy of the subject, which weighed down Georg Lukács' paradigm-forming studies on *History and Class Consciousness*[9] with heavy ballast from the philosophy of history.[10]

Radical critique of knowledge, as I had explained in the preface to *Knowledge and Human Interests*, is possible only in the form of social theory; in developing this idea there, however, I still tried to explain the normativity of knowledge and the analytical power of self-reflection in terms of a learning subject writ large. Consequently, the detranscendentalization of the achievements of this subject led only to a natural history of the 'human species'. It was not without reason that Apel described our shared conception of cognitive interests as a form of 'anthropological epistemology'. Hegel had already toppled Kant's transcendental subject from its noumenal pedestal and relocated it within the historical development of objective spirit or culture; and Marx has transferred the ethical life of culture into the material reproduction of society. But neither thinker had broken free from the conceptual apparatus of the philosophy of the subject: for Hegel and Marx, the learning process of world history takes place *in* large-scale subjects such as 'peoples' or 'social classes'. The idea of a history of the species that was no longer supposed to unfold only in forms of socially organized labour, but simultaneously as a communicatively mediated process of cultural formation, also remained captive to the model of subject-philosophy. The decisive step taken in the Gauss Lectures was to replace transcendental consciousness (as the source of the constitution of social relations) with everyday communicative practices that secure for society the same 'immanent reference to truth'. Without a reference to reason in its basic concepts, the (as it is now called) 'communication theory of society' would lack from the outset the nonarbitrary standard it requires to perform its continuing task of critically evaluating social pathologies. Of course, reason must be situated in social space and historical time. But in order to avoid achieving the detranscendentalization of the mind at the cost of introducing higher-level collective subjects, the challenge was now to 'found sociology in the theory of language' in a way that does justice to the decentring power of communication while also conceiving of the collective identities of societies and cultures as higher-level and condensed forms of intersubjectivity and taking into account the pluralistic character of social life. I will discuss the Gauss Lectures at somewhat greater length because they mark a turning point in my theoretical development.

(1) I undertook the overdue 'reconfiguration' of the basic concepts of social theory with reference to those individualistic approaches – such as Edmund Husserl's and Alfred Schütz's social phenomenology and the neo-Kantian sociology of Georg Simmel and Max Adler – which assume a plurality of transcendental subjects and therefore have to postulate necessary subjective conditions of possible socialization. To be sure, these transcendental approaches remain epistemologies doing duty as social theories, because they conceive of the reproduction of society as analogous to the production of an

intersubjectively shared world of possible experiences: from this epistemological perspective, the 'constitution' of a shared social world depends on the synthetic acts of consciousness of individual subjects. Despite these weaknesses, these theories served at the time as a bridge for the conception of society I had in mind as something which is not only networked through communication but is also *constructed* on the basis of acts of communication *rich in normative presuppositions*.

All that I had to do to bring the rationality potential of everyday communication into play was to replace the 'acts of cognition' of the subject of knowledge with the speech acts of acting subjects and to trace the production of meaning back, not to the constitution of the experiential world of conscious monads, but to communication in communities of language users. This establishes a relationship between communicative reason, on the one hand, and the conditions of social reproduction, on the other, *through the binding force of factually recognized validity claims*. At that time, I was trying a rather clumsy way to clarify 'the peculiarity of factually effective meaning structures':

Every society that we conceive of as a meaningfully structured system of life has an immanent relation to truth. For the reality of meaning structures is based on the peculiar facticity of claims to validity: In general, these claims are naively accepted – that is, they are jointly presumed to be fulfilled. But validity claims can, of course, be called into question. They raise a claim to validity, and this claim can be problematized: It can be confirmed or rejected. We can speak of 'truth' here only in the broad sense of the legitimacy of a claim that can be fulfilled or disappointed. Thus we say, for example, that an opinion or assertion, as well as a hope, wish, or guess, is correct or justified, that a promise or announcement has been properly made, that advice has

been honorably given, that a measure has been properly
taken, a description or an evaluation correctly done. In
everyday interactions, we rely naively on an unsurvey-
able wealth of such claims to legitimacy. It is always
only individual claims that emerge from this background and that are thematized and checked in case of
disappointment.[11]

Structuralism also presents language as a model for
a decentred, subjectless conception of society. But the
system of grammatical rules as such does not give rise
to any relation to truth; the latter first comes into play
with communication about states of affairs. The syntac-
tic dimension of language must be supplemented with
the semantic and pragmatic dimensions. If one person
wants to reach an understanding with another person
about something in the world, their communication can
also fail due to incomprehension or misunderstanding,
hence due to grammatical errors or because they lack a
shared language; but the actual, illocutionary goal – that
is, reaching understanding with another person about
what one *says* to the other person – can be missed only
at the semantic and pragmatic levels. From the perspective of a sociologist observing everyday practice, the
goal of communication is not to understand a spoken
utterance per se, but *to reach an understanding about
what was said*. A speaker misses this goal if she cannot
convince the addressee, *if she lacks reasons to dispel
doubts*. Inferential semantics (which I would only discover later, thanks to Robert Brandom) is based on this
very point: because participants in communication are
oriented to the goal of reaching understanding, they
always move within a space of reasons by which they let
themselves be influenced.

It was only later that I dealt with semantic questions.
Starting from hermeneutics, I initially followed the
path leading to formal pragmatics (to which inferential

semantics also ultimately leads). Still very much following in Karl-Otto Apel's footsteps, in *On the Logic of the
Social Sciences* I had dealt with the problem of how to
understand meaning in the work of both Gadamer and
the later Wittgenstein. By introducing this methodological problem into the theory of action and relating
it to the nodes of the communicative network of social
interactions, the latter acquire a different, constructive
theoretical status. Connecting the communicative model
of society with the phenomenological and neo-Kantian
theories of the constitution of society makes it clear that
a social scientific observer to whom only a hermeneutic
mode of access to her meaningfully structured object
domain is open is operating at *the same* level as the
actors she observes who both produce and reproduce
society – and thus the object domain of theories in the
social sciences – through their linguistically mediated
interactions.[12]

The communicative model of society inherits from
the transcendental conceptual strategy the levelling of
the gap that natural science maintains between theory
and object. The interpreting social scientist has a similar status to that of the subjects she observes. She can
make her observations and understand the data she
collects only in the role of a virtual participant. But, as
a result, the hermeneutical insights into the activity of
interpretation acquire direct relevance for describing
the interpretive practice of the acting subjects themselves. The communicative performances that bear the
burden of coordinating action in the field of observed
social interactions exhibit the same pattern as the
interpretations of the social scientific interpreter.

The Gauss Lectures are the result of a treatment of
basic concepts that led me from the Weberian notion of
norm-guided action via Mead's concept of symbolically
mediated interaction to the concept of 'communicative action'. This expression remained problematic as

long as the levels of social actions and of the speech acts performed in the execution of these actions were not clearly distinguished and the action-coordinating binding or bonding force of speech acts remained unexplained. This changed only with the reflections on formal pragmatics that I outlined in the fourth lecture. At that time, Noam Chomsky's theory of depth grammar, which claims to reconstruct the linguistic ability of competent speakers in terms of the rules for generating well-formed sentences, served me as a methodological guide for a theory of communicative competence. After having 'discovered' Chomsky as a critic of Skinnerian linguistic behaviourism on my first trip to America in 1965, I was impressed by the approach that reconstructs the know-how of competent speakers. However, I was less interested in linguistic competence as such. Something else was of central importance for me already at that time[13] – namely, the double structure of speech acts and the peculiar self-referentiality of everyday communication to which John Searle's speech act theory[14] had alerted me: 'A situation where it is possible to reach a mutual understanding requires that at least two speaker-hearers simultaneously establish communication at *both* levels: at the level of intersubjectivity, where the subjects talk with one another, and at the level of the objects (or states of affairs) *about* which they communicate.'[15]

Three further steps were required in order to grasp 'the life process of society as a generative process mediated by speech acts':[16]

- The illocutionary component formed with the aid of performative verbs had to be reassigned, as it were, as the seat of discursively redeemable validity claims. As a result, the illocutionary speech acts, which J.L. Austin had initially analysed with reference to the example of institutionally bound speech acts, undergo a functional transformation that goes beyond Searle's generalization.

- Based on a system of validity claims (to truth, truthfulness and rightness), which at the same time were intended to clarify the rational internal structure of everyday communication – i.e., the concept of 'communicative reason' – the speech acts had to be differentiated according to corresponding classes (constatives, expressives and regulatives) and examined with regard to their potential coupling effect for connecting the actions of different actors. The theory of speech acts, which plays the role of a theory of meaning in Searle, was now intended to explain a pragmatic mechanism for coordinating action.

- Communicative action, i.e. the type of social action characterized by a symmetrical use of speech acts oriented to reaching an understanding, had furthermore to be distinguished from the reflexive level of discourse on which the participants thematize validity claims that have become problematic. The discursive redemption of truth claims, which I examined in connection with the work of Stephen Toulmin on argumentation,[17] served as a model that I developed – somewhat prematurely, as it turned out[18] – into a consensus theory of truth.[19]

Considering the five lectures delivered at Princeton as a whole, it becomes apparent that these conceptual analyses provide at best the silverware but not the meal. But the formal pragmatic approach to communication (based on the mutual recognition of claims to validity) as the essential medium for generating social order provided me with a key to answering basic questions of social theory. The pair of concepts 'reaching understanding' vs. 'goal-orientation', which refer to opposed mechanisms of action coordination, opens up the whole field of sociological concepts of action (2).

The complementary relationship between communicative action and the lifeworld enables the step from action theory to social theory (3). Then three further problems can be clarified with the help of reflections from the theory of communication: the classical question of the relationship between the individual and society is answered in terms of a theory of intersubjectivity (4), Weber's concept of societal rationalization is extended beyond the aspect of purposive rationality (5) and the hermeneutic approach of interpretive sociology is deepened through a procedure of rational reconstruction (6). Finally, the theory of rationality forms a bridge between the *philosophical* discourse of modernity and the diagnosis of the present in *social theory* (7).

(2) With 'communicative action', the Gauss Lectures single out a highly improbable form of interaction. The connection between the actions of ego and those of alter is always jeopardized by the possibility of a criticizable validity claim being rejected. But the orientation to a theory of communication leads, starting from philosophical theories of action primarily concerned with explaining the teleological structure of purposive activity and rational choice, to sociological action theory, which aims at the interactive generation of social orders. The *Theory of Communicative Action* explains 'reaching understanding' as such a mechanism for coordinating action.[20]

The motivating force of a speech act offer is not a function of the validity of what is said, but of the credibility of the implicit guarantee provided by the speaker's offer to redeem the claim she has raised if necessary. It is the credibility of this guarantee that facilitates coordination. Furthermore, speech act theory offers viewpoints from which the unity in the diversity of sociological concepts of action becomes apparent. Social action ranges from 'rational choice' through 'strategic' and 'norm-guided' action to 'dramaturgical' action. These types of action can be differentiated according to the 'world references' that speakers adopt with first-, second- and third-person attitudes, respectively. Because the complexity of modern societies exceeds the internal perspective of theories of action, however, linguistic communication (together with values and norms) as a source of 'social solidarity' has to be *supplemented* by the media 'power' and 'market' as further mechanisms of systemic integration. 'Action steered by media' is a reaction to the high level of independence of economies steered by capital and of administrations steered by power.

(3) In the Gauss Lectures, it remained open how the formal pragmatic concept of communicative *action* can be developed into an empirically applicable communication theory *of society*. In the essay 'Actions, Speech Acts, Linguistically Mediated Interactions, and the Lifeworld', I tried to secure the continuity of the basic concepts by moving from the level of social action to the level of social order.[21] The concept of the lifeworld as the linguistically structured 'background' of communicative action is of central importance for this connection between the theory of action and social theory. Here, once again the work of Searle, who had interpreted Husserl's concept of the lifeworld in linguistic terms, proved to be helpful.[22] In a given context, the *literal* meaning of the standardized linguistic expressions must be tacitly supplemented by an antecedent, holistic, implicit 'know-how' that functions in the mode of certainties. Above all, this background of intersubjectively shared taken-for-granted assumptions explains why the lifeworld can absorb the risk of dissension that is ever-present in communication mediated by criticizable validity claims.

But a series of additional steps are required to develop the concept of society as 'symbolically structured lifeworld' out of a formal pragmatic concept of the lifeworld:

- Formal pragmatics develops the picture of a lifeworld as something that can be reproduced through the communicative actions of its members as long as the participants in everyday communication draw in turn on the linguistically articulated lifeworld background. However, this circular process does not seal itself off in a narcissistic way against the experiences of communicative actors in their dealings with each other and in coping with a risky environment. The world-disclosing language made available in advance by the lifeworld is not immune to the retroactive revisionary power of inner-worldly learning processes stimulated by surprising experiences. Although the structure of this process first has to be elucidated in formal pragmatic terms from the participant perspective, it then provides a conceptual orientation for a social scientific observer who examines an existing sociocultural form of life at the empirical level as one among many 'lifeworlds'.

- The transition from the participant perspective of the philosopher who reconstructs the 'know-how' of competent speakers to the perspective of an objectifying social scientist is made possible by a differentiation which, based on types of speech acts and validity claims, breaks down the opaque lifeworld background into interpretive schemes (cultural knowledge), legitimately ordered interpersonal relationships (resources of social solidarity) and personality structures (products of socialization), and thereby makes it accessible to empirical study.[23]

- Taking as a model the distinction between 'social and systemic integration', which are conceptually linked via the theory of action, the social scientific concept of system can be connected with that of the lifeworld.[24] The social relations steered by the media of 'power' and the 'market' can also assume the form of linguistically mediated interactions; but the actors, as rational participants in these subsystems, regularly pursue practical goals based on individual preferences.[25]

(4) Furthermore, the communications approach provides a solution to a problem that Husserl failed to solve under the premises of the philosophy of consciousness. In the *Cartesian Meditations*, he was not able to show how an intersubjectively shared lifeworld can be generated from the egological perspective of the transcendental monads of several 'original egos'.[26] This philosophical question, which underlies the paradigm dispute between mentalism and the philosophy of language, is also decisive for the issue in social theory that I have addressed in greater detail elsewhere[27] – namely, how the relationship between the individual and society can be understood.

In the tradition of American pragmatism influenced by Hegel, George Herbert Mead developed the concept of intersubjectivity out of the conditions of emergence of symbolically mediated interactions. According to Mead, symbols, by performing the decisive pragmatic function of coordinating action through reciprocal behavioural expectations, establish a shared understanding of the semantic content of these symbols among the actors involved. The pragmatic success of interaction-regulating symbols that assume *the same* meaning for both sides explains the semantic core of joint practices from which an intersubjectively shared understanding of the world arises.

Mead connects this – by no means primarily language-theoretical, but instead interactionist – approach to the intersubjectivity of the communication between alter and ego through expected behaviour with the ontogenesis of the developing person's relation to himself or herself. This ingenious connection allows him to develop the relationship between the individual and society in a dialectical way. As she becomes socialized, the adolescent develops into an irreplaceable acting subject and a unique individual by growing into more and more complex relationships of her social environment and learns to master ever more abstract roles with increasing degrees of reflexivity and corresponding distance from self. This difficult idea of individuation through socialization, which can be traced back to the young Hegel, can be rendered more precise with the instruments of formal pragmatics in terms of the meanings that performatively accompany the use of the first-person pronoun 'I'.

(5) The reflections in social theory about the social pathologies that arise in the course of cultural and social modernization processes are not thematized in philosophical contexts.[28] The question of the appropriate standards for criticizing a form of modernization that has become derailed is different. I have tried to derive such a normative foundation from aspects of the rationality of action,[29] so that it is advisable to recall briefly the relevant socioevolutionary background of the question. Following Max Weber's theory of social rationalization, older critical theory focused on symptoms of purposive rationality that has become independent from its functional context (an analysis later honed into the diagnosis of a 'dialectic of enlightenment'). In the *Theory of Communicative Action*, this critique of 'instrumental reason' is replaced by a critique of 'functional reason', that is of a form of systemic rationality that has become independent from the communicative rationality of the lifeworld. In my view, the emergence of new systemic mechanisms and self-steering capacities depends on possibilities that first arise at evolutionary thresholds through a progressive *rationalization of the lifeworld*. Sociocultural development differs from *natural* evolution, which is a result of random variation and selection, insofar as it

depends on cumulative problem-solving and learning processes. Societies also *learn* by using the moral and legal conceptions contained in worldviews to develop more and more comprehensive forms of social integration.[30] In modern societies, the decoupling of system and lifeworld goes so far that the mere *mediatization* of the lifeworld can turn into *colonization*. Pathological effects occur whenever systemic imperatives intrude on the core areas of cultural reproduction, social integration and socialization to such an extent that the integrity of the symbolic reproduction of the lifeworld based on communicative action is undermined. 'Excessive' monetization or bureaucratization processes mean that the functional imperatives of economic or administrative systems are satisfied disproportionally at the expense of lifeworld resources of social solidarity.[31]

This diagnosis is based on a theory of social evolution as a series of steps,[32] which provides the groundwork for answering the question: 'what makes a form of life rational?'[33] The rationality potential of communicative action unfolds in a lifeworld whose rational internal structures form a counterweight to the functional imperatives of functional systems specifially when the latter reveal themselves only in symptoms of systematically distorted communication.[34]

(6) The Weberian understanding of modernization as social rationalization is based on the assumption that rational structures are embodied in space and time and that empirical studies can demonstrate that rational structures operate in social practices.[35] Social science must adopt a reconstructive approach when it confronts this demanding task. It has to uncover deep structures beneath the surface of the hermeneutically accessible diversity of symbolic expressions and objects. For example, if one wants to develop a history of science from this reconstructive perspective that explains why theories were accepted as convincing in their time,

then one needs a context-sensitive theory of science that describes the rational standards of research practices. In an analogous way a moral theory is needed to understand experimentally generated moral judgements as solutions to problems and the ontogenesis of corresponding capabilities as a learning process. Thus, Max Weber understood legal systems and the practices of the administration of justice or the theocentric and cosmological worldviews of the major world religions as more or less rational solutions to social conflicts or to basic existential needs.[36]

It is important in this context to contrast the methodological procedure of such reconstructions with the hermeneutic approach of the humanities.[37] The 'interpretative turn' of sociology, first proclaimed in the 1970s, provided me with an opportunity to stress that the social sciences, too, share a hermeneutic mode of access to their symbolically structured object domains. Then I drew upon insights from both philosophical hermeneutics and the philosophy of language to recall the performative character of the process of understanding and the participant perspective from which an interpreter approaches her object. This does not jeopardize the objectivity of understanding, because the interpreter can reach an impartial judgement also in the role of a virtual participant – as a participant in dialogue, as it were. Interpretation always takes place in the space of reasons and every interpretation is rational insofar as the interpreter has to weigh up the reasons that render the *interpretandum* understandable in the first place.

In this way, the rational character of interpretations reveals a rationality inherent in the symbolic objects, a rationality to which they lay claim and to which they sometimes fail to measure up. Unlike ordinary interpretation, a reconstruction does not aim directly at the meaning or content of a specific text or utterance, of a specific institution or mode of action, or of a social process or an artefact, be it a Biedermeier chair or an abstract painting. Rather, it takes aim at the rules in accordance with which these symbolic objects are generated and at the standards with reference to which they can be accepted as 'skilful' or criticized as defective.[38] Individuals who have mastered such generative rules and standards possess certain competences. In the vast majority of cases it is a question of cognitive, linguistic or practical competences as such – which have, after all, been the focus of conceptual analysis in philosophy since Plato's time.

It is philosophy, therefore, with its analyses of the intuitive 'know-how' that accompanies action only in an unthematized, performative way, which serves as the example of 'reconstructive understanding'. Philosophy explains the know-how involved in making true judgements and drawing correct conclusions, in producing grammatical sentences and using them correctly to communicate, in acting morally or rationally, in developing an authentic self-understanding, and so forth. But unlike philosophical reconstructions, empirically based reconstructive theories do not start from idealized examples of judgements, speech acts or actions; rather, they proceed from empirical phenomena *encountered* in a hermeneutically disclosed object-domain in order to understand them in terms of their enabling conditions and at the same time to evaluate them as more or less rational examples of their kind. This calls for a special division of labour between causally explanatory and reconstructive procedures, which I illustrate using the example of Kohlberg's theory of the development of moral consciousness in children and adolescents.

(7) Finally, the theory of communicative action not only provides the appropriate perspective for describing the problem of rationality taken up by Max Weber and essentially continued in Western Marxism. This

perspective also provides us with valuable insights into the origins of critical social theory in the critique of reason as practised from Kant to Hegel. The starting point is the challenge that a new, radicalized consciousness of time posed for philosophical thinking around 1800. This new experience of time forced philosophy, now in the guise of deflated postmetaphysical thinking, to address a completely new theme – namely, the self-understanding of modernity as presumably uncoupled from tradition. At the same time, the only remaining source of normative orientations after Kant was reason's critique of itself. The power of practical reason is now exhausted in rational law and rational morality. Whereas the classical teachings of the good life and the just society, ethics and politics, were still of a piece, postmetaphysical thinking no longer believes itself capable of singling out a *model of the common good as generally binding*.

At the same time, the new historical consciousness confronts philosophy with the multiplied contingencies of a future anticipated as something that needs to be shaped. It becomes even more acutely aware of the growing need for orientation the more categorically it rejects the demand for metaphysical answers. As the need for practical orientation becomes more acute in each present situation, therefore, philosophy acquires the new theme of 'capturing its time in thought' in addition to the familiar tasks of its classical disciplines. As I showed in a review of two traditions of social theory,[39] philosophy after Hegel understood the task of such an analysis of the present in terms of the critique of reason – but henceforth addressed it only in a division of labour with sociology, a discipline which first emerged around the same time. This development, which led via Hegel, Marx, Max Weber and Georg Lukács to the interdisciplinary research programme of early Critical Theory, reached its culmination in the self-referentially totalizing critique of reason of the *Dialectic of Enlightenment*.[40] This marked the end point of the historically influential format that Hegel had lent the problem of the self-understanding of modernity.

Today sociology seems to cultivate only half of this legacy. The two most successful theoretical approaches, rational choice theory and functionalist systems theory, maintain the claim to provide empirical explanations of Western modernization processes as a form of rationalization, but they conceive of the theory of rationality in narrower terms by separating it entirely from the context of modern moral and legal theory.[41] Heidegger, by contrast, inflated the legacy of the critique of reason by continuing the programme of a critique of modernity with other means – as did the late Wittgenstein and his contextualist followers. However, these orientations for postmodern diagnoses of the present provide starting points for cultural studies at best but not for social science.

Around the time of Hegel's death, the function of developing a self-understanding of modernity was transferred from philosophy to sociology,[42] instead of to other social sciences such as political economy, political science and constitutional law or anthropology.[43] Social theory in the classical sense owes its existence to a contingent constellation. Signs that this symbiosis is dissolving have become more evident, especially since the so-called 'cultural turn'. This is shown by the development of sociology itself. In the curriculum of the discipline, social theory has withdrawn into the confines of the 'classics' and has been historicized as a whole,[44] while a highly professionalized and internally differentiated expert community sees its relation to practice as being to provide empirically reliable advice to functional elites – and no longer to contribute to clarifying collective self-understanding in the classical sense. This may represent a loss for the discourse of modernity, but it is also an opportunity. The discourse of modernity would benefit from a philosophy that is open to unbiased cooperation with *all* of the human sciences. But if the function of forming a self-understanding becomes the preserve of a mode of philosophizing that seals itself off in a narcissistic way from a serious division of labour with empirical disciplines, then – as the decade of discussion of so-called postmodernism has shown – the door is wide open for dilettantism.[45]

2

Theory of Rationality and Theory of Meaning

I initially dealt with issues in the theory of discourse and the theory of meaning in the context of social theory. In the Hegelian-Marxist tradition, society was understood as a totality. But this conception was no longer appropriate for the decentred character of functionally differentiated societies, which are often described as 'heterarchical'. Moreover, I had to find a way to go beyond Horkheimer and Adorno's critique of reason that had become aporetic and to find a convincing justification for the normative foundations of critical social theory.[1] I responded to these two challenges with a 'linguistic turn' in Critical Theory that combines the perspectives of the theories of rationality and of language into a normatively charged conception of 'reaching mutual understanding about something in the world'. This approach was originally inspired at the methodological level by Noam Chomsky's approach to a theory of linguistic competence, at the level of formal semantics by John Searle's theory of speech acts and, when it came to the theory of rationality, by the controversy emerging from Oxford at the time over the correspondence theory of truth.[2]

The sociological context of my research explains the pragmatic approach: 'reaching an understanding' comes into view at this level as a mechanism for coordinating actions in interaction. Understanding a speech act represents just one link in the chain of communication connecting a speaker with an addressee who takes a "yes' or 'no' position. The two reciprocally interconnected acts – the utterance made by ego and the stance adopted by alter – are the elementary units of a form of communication that makes social action possible by 'connecting' complementary practical intentions. The linguistically mediated interaction that comes about as a result of the functional embedding of the communicative use of language in a context of social interaction I call 'communicative action'. Although this may have been a sufficient foundation for a critical social theory, the global concept of reaching understanding had to be analysed in greater detail. After completing the *Theory of Communicative Action* and returning to teaching philosophy at the university after a period of institutionalized research, I had the time to devote myself to theories of meaning, rationality and truth.[3] From the perspective of a theory of communicative reason, there is an internal relationship between the theory of language and meaning (I), different aspects of rationality that come together in the use of language oriented to reaching mutual understanding (II), and the discourse theory of truth (III). Finally, the formal-pragmatic understanding of the representational function of language has implications for ontology and epistemology (IV).

I. *Formal Pragmatics*

I began with a historical explanation of the concept of 'reaching understanding' in terms of the encounter of hermeneutics with analytical philosophy of language,[4] and went on to develop the formal pragmatic approach based on a critique of three competing theories of meaning.[5] Thanks to the rise of analytical philosophy, the philosophy of language in the guise of theories of meaning became one of the core philosophical disciplines during the twentieth century (although this emphasis has in the meantime shifted again since the death of Willard Van Orman Quine and Donald Davidson with the growing influence of cognitive science). The generation who studied in Germany immediately following the Second World War, however, found themselves at a crossroads where two analytical currents – which crystallized around Rudolf Carnap's philosophy of science and Ludwig Wittgenstein's recently published *Philosophical Investigations*, respectively – collided with philosophical hermeneutics. The most readily available option for us was connected with Martin Heidegger, who was the dominant figure on the philosophical scene at that time. With his 'turn' from existential ontology to the history of being, he had also accorded language a central role as the 'house of being', and even invested this 'mouthpiece of being' with diagnostic significance for understanding contemporary social and political developments.

From a historical point of view, this turn to the philosophy of language was marked by a twofold inheritance. On the one hand, Heidegger had appropriated the hermeneutic tradition leading via Droysen and Dilthey back to Schleiermacher and, on the other, he took up Humboldt's conception of linguistic worldviews when later on he stylized the ontological twists and turns of Western metaphysics into a 'destiny of being'. Karl-Otto Apel and I were first introduced into this world of the German Historical School by Erich Rothacker and subsequently became acquainted with the two above-mentioned currents in analytical philosophy. These latter traditions drew upon the shared source of Gottlob Frege's logical semantics, but they returned to post-war Germany from emigration in the United States and Great Britain as competitors.

My interest in the problem of how to understand linguistic meaning was connected with questions concerning the logic of the social sciences, which led me to deal with analytical philosophy of science. Charles Sanders Peirce's classical works on the logic of inquiry became particularly important,[6] because Peirce's Kantian pragmatism highlights the misleading step in abstraction that a purely methodological use of logical semantics compels us to make. Carnap subjects theoretical languages to a logical analysis, while he excludes the rule-governed practice of inquiry from the domain of rational reconstruction and leaves it to empirical studies. His formal analysis comes to a halt before it could actually start at the pragmatic level. As a result, the cooperation of the community of investigators, which was central to Peirce's logic of inquiry, loses the dignity of rational, rule-governed practices in which the constitution of the object domains of different scientific disciplines is also rooted. Karl-Otto Apel's transcendental pragmatics is based on the hermeneutic recovery of this dimension.[7] Similarly, Albrecht Wellmer's critique of Karl Popper's *Logic of Scientific Discovery* takes issue with the same semantic abstractions from the rational core of the pragmatics of research.[8]

On the other hand, Wittgenstein's later philosophy offered itself as a point of comparison with Heidegger's hermeneutics. Wittgenstein's analysis of language games drew attention to the pragmatic dimension of language use. He conceived of linguistic understanding as a practical ability acquired through initiation into a linguistically structured form of life. From this perspective, the constructive epistemic activities of the transcendental subject are desublimated and expanded into the 'detranscendentalized', but still rule-governed, practices of subjects capable of speech and action who are now *situated in the world*. From the perspective of a detranscendentalization of the constructive achievements of transcendental consciousness that Kant transposed into the noumenal realm, there are unmistakable parallels between Wittgenstein's pluralism of language games that extend *into social space* and Heidegger's *historical* sequence of ontologically or grammatically pre-structured interpretations of the world. Both authors attribute to grammar (in Wittgenstein's sense) or to the ontology of language (in Heidegger's sense) a world-generating spontaneity, that is, the power to structure diverse forms of life and to make epochal worldviews accessible. Karl-Otto Apel was one of the first philosophers to propose the now common juxtaposition of these two most influential twentieth-century philosophies.[9]

These two complementary – hermeneutic and analytical – versions of the linguistic turn explain the development of the formal pragmatic conception of 'mutual understanding' based on a critical assimilation of those traditions that go back to Humboldt and Frege. For Heidegger and Wittgenstein, languages possess a world-forming spontaneity that is similar to the spontaneity of the transcendental subject. However, both thinkers immunize the world-disclosing function of languages and the grammar of forms of life against the revisionary power of learning processes *within the world*. The critique of the primacy of this 'apriori of meaning' reminds us of the force and logic of 'conversation' and argumentation to which Humboldt already accorded independent weight vis-à-vis the perspective-generating selectivity of linguistic worldviews.

The stubborn rational character of communication is based both on what actors learn from their efforts *to cope* with the world and on what participants in discourse learn *from each other*. The categorial pre-understanding advanced by a world-disclosing language is subject to the revisionary pressure of new empirical knowledge acquired through learning processes. This speaks in favour of a pragmatic approach to the analysis of the relationship between meaning and validity that develops Michael Dummett's epistemic truth semantics further. In essence, the formal pragmatic theory of meaning states that the addressee understands an utterance if he knows the conditions that make the validity claim raised with this utterance rationally acceptable.

I develop this thesis through a critique of three theories of meaning, which understand the meaning of a linguistic expression, respectively,

- from the perspective of what is meant as 'intentional meaning', or
- from the perspective of what has been said as 'propositional meaning', or
- from the perspective of its use as 'utterance meaning' in a context of action.[10]

Each of these semantic approaches focuses on one function of language and abstracts from the context, which I illustrate using Karl Bühler's three-function scheme of language (which serves at the same time as an expression of the speaker's intention, as the representation of a state of affairs and as an appeal to the addressee to take up and enter in a special relation with the speaker). Although speech act theory embraces all of these functional aspects, the limits of the semantic version of this theory are made apparent by John Searle's attempt to develop an adequate classification of speech acts.[11] It is the formal pragmatic interpretation of the understanding of propositions as a function of communication that first highlights the three equally original dimensions of communicating 'what one means' 'with others' 'about something'. Thus, there is a *threefold* relationship between the meaning of a linguistic expression and what is meant by it, how it is used and what is said in it.

To these dimensions correspond the validity claims of

the 'serious' or 'sincere' expression of intentions or experiences, of the production of normatively 'appropriate' or 'correct' interpersonal relations and of the 'true' representation of states of affairs. If we examine how speech acts can be negated *as a whole* (rather than in their individual components or presuppositions), we arrive at precisely these three validity claims to truthfulness, rightness and truth, which are geared to intersubjective recognition, but are at the same time criticizable. The orientation to validity claims belongs to the pragmatic conditions of *possible* communication because the illocutionary goal of the use of language oriented to reaching understanding is measured by whether the addressee can accept the validity *claim* raised by the speaker. Of course, a theory of meaning is only intended to clarify the conditions of *understanding* of linguistic expressions. But the *primary* goal of the communicative use of language is that members of a linguistic community should *reach an understanding* about something in the world that they encounter from within the horizon of their lifeworld. Therefore, the conditions of understanding a linguistic expression refer to the conditions of the possible mutual understanding of something in the world achiev*able* with the aid of that expression. Understanding an expression means knowing how (under what conditions) one *could* use it to communicate with someone and reach an understanding of something.

If we now understand the goal of reaching understanding as 'rationally motivated' agreement (which applies to the paradigmatic case of understanding of what is or is not the case), then an extension and generalization of Michael Dummett's *empirical interpretation* of truth semantics to all three of the validity claims mentioned above suggests itself. The meaning of an utterance is explained in terms of its conditions of validity; however, we cannot ignore the conditions under which a speaker could specify reasons for why the validity conditions are fulfilled and a listener could recognize them. The claim to validity that a speaker raises for what is said towards a hearer is based on such reasons. In the process, the speaker appeals implicitly to a corresponding potential of reasons on which he thinks he can rely if the addressee rejects his claim to validity. These reasons *interpret* the conditions of validity and to that extent belong themselves to the conditions that make an expression acceptable. In the case of expressive speech acts, the reasons in question are, of course, indirect ones, because the truthfulness of a speaker's self-representation can ultimately be verified only by the consistency of the actions to which it gives rise.

In the case of constative and regulative speech acts, however, understanding the utterance involves knowing *the kind of reasons* with which a speaker could redeem his claim to validity in discourse, that is in the course of a rule-governed exchange of reasons. This is also the point of departure for a version of inferential semantics that can be traced back to Wilfrid Sellars[12] and draws attention to the network of logical relations implied in the vocabulary (and thus to the world-disclosing function of everyday language and to the corresponding articulation of the lifeworld background). If we keep in mind the complex requirement of rationally motivated agreement with a criticizable validity claim, the formal pragmatic theory of meaning can be boiled down to the following rule of thumb: we understand an utterance when we know what makes it rationally acceptable (and what practical consequences follow when it is accepted).

II. Communicative Rationality

For the theory of meaning, the understanding of a linguistic utterance is the *explanandum*. As an *explanans*,

formal pragmatics uses the concept of 'rational acceptability' in the sense of a warranty for the 'discursive
redemption' of truth claims and of validity claims
analogous to truth. Obviously, this *explanans* is itself
in need of explanation. This does not necessarily lead
to a vicious circle, however, if we base such a theory
of communicative rationality in turn on insights from
language pragmatics. Specifying validity claims in terms
of classes of performative verbs, for example, provides
a guideline for examining the discourses and patterns of
argumentation with whose help the validity claims can
be redeemed. The theory of rationality and the theory of
meaning support each other.

Starting from a discussion with Herbert Schnädelbach,
I examine the connection between rationality and reaching understanding and suggest that 'communicative
rationality' should be understood as one of three 'roots'
of rationality.[13] From the beginning, the philosophical
tradition dealt with the *epistemic rationality* of statements, the *teleological rationality* of actions and the
ethical and *moral rationality* of a *good* conduct of life or
a *just* practice, respectively. The meaning of the rationality of utterances and modes of conduct *refers* to the
truth of statements and to the success of interventions or
to the success of value orientations and to the justice of
norms. However, rationality is *measured* directly only
in terms of *the available reasons* which, in a given case,
suggest that a state of affairs can be represented or a
purpose realized, that a life plan is not a failure or that
a practice is just. Opinions or intentions, conceptions
of the good life or just actions are 'rational' if they are
supported by good reasons – regardless of whether they
are true or effective or of whether they are ultimately
appropriate or right.

Reasons are no more a private possession than is
language itself; in cases of controversy, whether reasons
are good or bad can be determined only in the forum

of a rule-governed exchange of arguments. Therefore, the practice of argumentation, which requires the participants to adopt a reflexive attitude towards validity claims that have become problematic, is the key to a complex form of rationality in which those different forms of rationality mentioned come together and merge. Such a practice calls for a demanding form of communication, which can be understood in turn as a reflexive form of communicative action. Therefore, discursive rationality refers to an origin in the 'communicative rationality' built into action oriented to validity itself. Tracing the unifying power of the speech oriented to reaching understanding manifested in the insightful acceptance of validity claims – and ultimately based on the 'unforced force' of the better argument – we arrive at the telos inscribed in this rationality, namely, *rationally motivated agreement*.

The text mentioned in the previous footnote deals essentially with the question of how the different forms of rationality fit together. Because ethical and moral questions refer to the life orientations and practical orientations of *socialized* individuals and depend intrinsically on discursive clarification, we can understand practical reason as derivative of communicative rationality. This practical reason need not concern us here, because it does not represent a 'root' in its own right independent of communicative reason. Things are different with the *rationality* of *knowledge* and of *purposive activity*. The epistemic and teleological core structures can be grasped in *statements* and *intentions*. Thus, they are incorporated in the logical semantics of a language and can be analysed in terms of corresponding sentences or thoughts. That these two *roots* of epistemic and teleological rationality possess a certain independence is suggested by the fact that they find different embodiments in complementary, but *equally important* functions of language use, representation and communication, *and equally* in corresponding components of communicative action, where language use is based on the teleological structure of action. This certain independence of the two 'roots' of rationality is also reflected in a certain semantic self-sufficiency of assertoric and intentional sentences. *Having* beliefs and practical intentions does not seem to be *internally* connected with a communicative *use* of language. However, the rationality of this 'having' *calls for* reflection on the validity of corresponding propositional and intentional sentences. Because thoughts entertained *in foro interno* can be understood as a reflection of a public exchange of arguments, here we again encounter the discursive rationality with which every use of language and every action, whether communicative or not, is interwoven.

However, the pluralistic picture of three independent roots of rationality that coalesce to form discursive rationality assigns communicative rationality an ancillary status. This could have disturbing consequences for a theory which assumes that the telos of reaching understanding is inherent in linguistic communication as such. A relevant objection in this connection is that the meaning of assertoric and intentional sentences can be explained exclusively in terms of conditions of truth or success, without having to leave the semantic level. This is the intuition to which all semantic theories since Frege appeal that reduce speech acts to just two directions of fit between proposition and state of affairs. The correct response to this objection is that the very meaning of the truth and success conditions of propositions can be explained only in terms of the possible embedding of these propositions in acts of asserting propositions or of announcing an intended action. Just as truth conditions, which are publicly examinable *and are therefore in need of interpretation*, can be understood *as* truth conditions only in the light of the assertoric meaning of assertions, so too the meaning of publicly examinable *success* conditions also becomes accessible only from the point of view of *declared* or *announced* intentions (or of requests that have an inherently public character). We understand the meaning of assertoric or intentional sentences only in the light of the performatively raised claim to validity (that the corresponding truth conditions are fulfilled) or the performatively announced intention (that the actor will fulfil the corresponding success conditions or calls upon an addressee to fulfil them).

However, another observation speaks against this heightening of the concept of *reaching understanding* into the telos of *agreement*: intentional sentences can also be used in normatively freestanding announcements and demands that lack institutional support or any other kind of normative background support in habit, morality or law. Without an *authorizing background*, expressions of will, which can *only* be attributed to the actor himself, have a special status within the class of regulative speech acts. For such unauthorized announcements or imperatives do not raise a normative claim to validity. These speech acts claim to be 'rational' on other grounds and as a result to be 'rationally acceptable' for other participants in communication – specifically, on grounds that lend plausibility to the truthfulness of the actor and the feasibility of the intended action (the truth of the assumed conditions of practicability). Whereas normative reasons claim to be binding for both sides (and moral reasons even claim to bind all potentially affected persons), *actor-relative* reasons are sufficient to justify the seriousness of a practical intention – ones that a listener can ascribe to the speaker as good reasons, even if he does not share them.

This distinctive feature has forced me to make a differentiation within the concept of illocutionary success. Only in the case of assertoric and normative validity claims is illocutionary success measured by an agreement based on actor-independent – i.e., intersubjectively shared – reasons. (In the case of truthfulness and authenticity claims, indirect confirmation by consistent action takes the place of such reasons.) In contrast, illocutionary success in cases of normatively non-embedded announcements and imperatives – similar to expressing an opinion that is assumed to be only subjectively correct – is measured exclusively by whether convincing actor-relative reasons can be attributed to the speaker. For the formal pragmatic theory of meaning, which asserts a connection between understanding an utterance and knowledge of its acceptability conditions, this revision does not entail any fundamental corrections, but it does for the theory of action.

The distinction between communication aimed at a rationally motivated agreement and communication about the actor-relative rationality of utterances implies a gradation of the illocutionary binding force that language can have for social action. The use of language 'oriented to *agreement*' has a more powerful coordinating effect than language use 'oriented to *reaching understanding*'. Corresponding to these are strong and weak forms of communicative action. In both cases, the presuppositions of communicative action remain intact – namely, the assumption of a shared objective world, the orientation to validity claims and the reciprocal imputation of rationality and accountability. On the other hand, the use of language oriented to consequences in strategic interactions or in indirect forms of 'leading somebody to understand' is subject to the conditions of teleological rationality; however, it is parasitic on a form of linguistic understanding that must be *acquired* performatively in contexts of communicative action. Only participation in practices embedded in the lifeworld opens the door to the semantic wealth of a language.

The spectrum of the different modes of language

use and of the different types of action reaches beyond the core area of communicative action. The telos of reaching understanding is inherent neither in language as such nor in action as such. Only in the spotlight of the intersubjectively shared lifeworlds of social groups capable of acting collectively do language and action *combine* to form the use of language oriented to *reaching understanding* and *communicative* action.[14] And only within this horizon can semantic potentials be formed and transformed out of the interaction between a world-disclosing language that articulates the lifeworld background and the learning processes of subjects capable of speech and action who have to cope with the contingencies of occurrences in the world.

The linguistic disclosure of the world stands in a complementary relationship to the rational achievements of fallible subjects in the world who are capable of learning. A text I wrote in honour of my friend Tom McCarthy deals with the idea of the detranscendentalization of a 'performative' subjectivity that expresses itself in the cognitive dynamics of the reproduction of the lifeworld through communicative action.[15] The constructive activity of reason operates in the spontaneous accomplishments of a form of communicative action that derives it support from the taken-for-granted background of a performatively present, linguistically articulated lifeworld. In this way, communicative reason retains something of the transcendental heritage of *world-forming spontaneity*. Whereas the lifeworld background consists of implicit knowledge that is particular in nature, detranscendentalized reason preserves its *universal legislative authority* by withdrawing into the inconspicuous, but general and unavoidable pragmatic presuppositions of communicative action. The rational interior of communicative action compels the actors to make assumptions that they *have to* make simply by engaging in this practice. These are not general and necessary conditions in the strictly transcendental sense, but general presuppositions of a communicative practice that are de facto unavoidable, because there are no functional equivalents in known sociocultural forms of life.

Detranscendentalized reason dispersed in diverse life-world contexts leaves traces of a general legislation in the counterfactual content of unavoidable presuppositions of communication. Communicative actors must (in a weak sense of transcendental necessitation) start from context-transcending pragmatic presuppositions, which are taken for granted until the contrary is demonstrated:

- the participants ascribe rationality and accountability to each other;
- they assume that they speak a common language and use its expressions with identical meanings;
- they assume that there is a shared objective world of things existing independently of any description;
- they take their orientation here and now from context-transcending validity claims; and
- they presuppose that assertoric and normative validity claims can be redeemed in discourse.

Through these presuppositions of the communicative use of language, the normative constitution of the human mind has a shaping influence on the social reality of the environment in which it operates.

In the tradition that bypasses Kant and draws *directly* on Hume, the idea of a desublimated form of reason embodied in the communicative practice of everyday life is met with incomprehension. Empiricism has a hard time with idealizations, and even more so with the *empirical role* played by the *counterfactual presuppositions* of communicative action *in the everyday construction of social reality*. That is why I do not limit myself in the above-mentioned text to analysing these presuppositions, but also try to establish an affinity, and even a genealogical connection, between the pragmatic idealizations and the Kantian theory of ideas. The second part of that essay supplements the part on Kant's theory of ideas with a demonstration that the analytical theories of meaning from Gottlob Frege to Michael Dummett and Robert Brandom cannot do without idealizations either. In Donald Davidson these idealizations assume the form of methodological postulates. Moreover, the example of triangulation, with reference to which Davidson undertakes a conceptual reconstruction of the origin of elementary linguistic meanings, shows that the strategy of constructing theories of meaning on the model of empirical theories is doomed to failure. The reconstruction of the know-how of competent speakers cannot break out of the circle of the speakers' own linguistic preunderstanding.

III. Discourse Theory of Truth

The connection between rationality and meaning can also be explained differently as a consequence of the turn to the pragmatics of language. If the linguistic constitution of the human mind keeps us in the space of reasons and prevents us from adopting an observer stance somewhere between language and reality, then we cannot have *direct* access to conditions of the validity of utterances. We can redeem cheques that we issue on the truth of a statement, for example, only in the currency of reasons. Even though good reasons only prove the rationality of a claim to truth, there is no other way to establish the truth of a statement. Since I wanted to explain the concept of communicative rationality in terms of the features of argumentation that justify the presumption that its results are rational, the controversy over concepts of truth being conducted at the time by prominent figures (F.P. Ramsey, J.L. Austin, P.F. Strawson, Michael Dummett and John Searle) provided a good starting point. I first dealt with this discussion in a Festschrift published for Walter Schulz. This text goes back to 1970[16] and is quite speculative; it contains over-hasty theses that I was later forced to retract. A short time later, I took up the core idea of a consensus theory of truth at the end of the Gauss Lectures. This premature text on theories of truth nevertheless contains orientations that have become important for the architecture of my theory as a whole.

The critique of the *correspondence* theory of truth is based in essence on the objection to a reification of facts. The existence of states of affairs must not be assimilated to the existence of objects about which states of affairs are asserted. But if the concept of a fact, as Peirce already recognized, can be explained only by recourse to the truth of statements, the correspondence between proposition and fact does not offer a suitable starting point for explaining the relationship between statements and a reality independent of language. In contrast, I find the pragmatist conception convincing according to which our primary dealings with the objects existing in the world are not at the level of discourses, but instead 'in practical and experiential contexts' – hence, not where problematic truth claims are thematized but where they are taken at face value.

This is why I make a distinction between action and discourse. The level of action is characterized both by naïve anticipatory interpretations and certainties and by disappointed expectations that can trigger learning processes. The level of discourse, by contrast, frees us from the constraints of action and the pressure of experience, and allows us to adopt a hypothetical stance on taken-for-granted assumptions that have become problematized in the meantime. This differentiation also disqualifies certainties based on perception and belief as paradigms for explaining truth. We raise truth claims for propositions that can in principle be true *or* false. The *evidence theory* of truth fails to take into account the fact that the concept of truth is interwoven with that of fallible knowledge. The concept of the lifeworld as a background of performatively present certainties (which was still lacking at the time of the essay) would have lent even greater precision to the contrast between truth and evidence.

The *consensus theory* of truth that I favoured at the time is based on the observation that there cannot be any knock-down arguments, only more or less 'good' arguments, in substantive controversies. On the one hand, the standards in terms of which reasons are weighed are not immune to criticism either. On the other hand, simple perceptual evidence does provide strong, but not *compelling* reasons, because it can function as a source of reasons only in the form of contestable perceptual protocols. If we want to uphold the everyday intuition of a *realist* epistemology, the discursive redemption of truth claims must nevertheless be possible. Hence, the burden of justification shifts from the content of the reasons to the process of selecting what in each case count as the better reasons. This procedural version of a discursive concept of truth builds on the differential weight of the decisive reasons: those propositions prove to be true that continually withstand objections in discourses. The concept of truth can put a stop to the infinite regress in virtue of the well-founded assumption that the unforced force of the better argument will ultimately prevail in discourses.

The point of reference for differentiating a *justifying* consensus from a merely *factually achieved* understanding are the demanding pragmatic presuppositions of rational discourse under which a potential consensus is supposed to come about. The formal pragmatic point of this theory of truth consists in the assumption that these presuppositions of argumentation can be reconstructed – that is, *proved* – in a similar way to the *weak* 'transcendental' presuppositions of communicative action. Anyone who engages without reservation in a practice of argumentation must assume that the given communication situation approximates sufficiently to the conditions of an 'ideal speech situation'. I have often regretted this misleading formulation and have repeatedly revoked it. It is not in any way intended to suggest the utopian 'prefiguration of a form of life'; rather, it refers only to the fulfilment of *idealized conditions of justification*, specifically,

- publicity and inclusion,
- equal participation,
- the exclusion of illusion and deception, and
- immunization against external and internal constraints.

In qualifying their status, I emphasize the essential critical function of these idealizations, which acquire an additional regulative function when it comes to the legal *institutionalization* of discourses, for example, in teaching and research or in parliaments and courts.

The controversy that I conducted over many years with my friend Richard Rorty finally led me to correct the consensus theory of truth I had originally advocated on the crucial point that it neglects the difference between truth and justifiable assertability.[17] My contribution to a volume of discussions with Rorty edited by Robert Brandom[18] also provided an occasion to rectify my previous neglect of the *coherence* and *deflationist* conceptions of truth. But the main focus of the controversy is on the contextualist levelling of the difference between 'truth' and 'justified assertability', which Rorty defended against Karl-Otto Apel, Hilary Putnam and myself. In the process I became aware of a motif that had initially misled me into advocating an undifferentiated version of the discourse theory of truth.

Moral theory during the first two post-war decades was dominated by noncognitivist conceptions, whereas I – like Paul Lorenzen and Karl-Otto Apel – argued against this mainstream in favour of an intersubjectivist version of Kantian deontology. This cognitivism could be justified without making concessions to moral realism if moral claims to validity were redeemable in the same way as assertoric validity claims. At the time, Steven Toulmin's scheme of argumentation[19] encouraged me to try to assimilate practical to theoretical discourse: 'If rightness can be classified as a discursively redeemable validity claim alongside truth, then it follows that correct norms must be justifiable in a similar way to true statements.'[20]

This motif led me to *over-generalize* the explanation offered by the consensus theory of the binding validity of norms, which I still understand as an epistemic mode of validity. However, the assimilation of the truth of statements to the validity of moral judgements and norms loses sight of the *justification-transcending* meaning of the truth of statements, which refer to things in an objective world independent of description. The 'warning' use of the truth predicate already reveals the difference in meaning between truth and justified assertability. The objections of Albrecht Wellmer and Cristina Lafont, together with a reflection of Donald Davidson's, ultimately compelled me to abandon an epistemic concept of truth. However, this revision affects only the consensus theory's *understanding* of truth, not the epistemic role that rational discourses play in the same way, if not to the same extent, in *redeeming* claims to truth as well as claims to rightness.

IV. On Epistemology

My early work on truth theories is at its least clear when it addresses epistemological questions. Already at that time, however, the appeal to progress in knowledge reflected in the 'adaptation' of linguistic and conceptual systems reveals the view that the discursive work of justification merely supplements the learning processes triggered by practical dealings with the world. In the introduction to *Truth and Justification*, therefore, I took up once again questions I had left to one side since *Knowledge and Human Interests*.[21] Taking the interconnection between the two central functions of language – namely, representation and communication – as my starting point, there I examine the realist epistemological meaning of the assumption of an 'objective world' and address the naturalistic question of how the normativity of a linguistically structured lifeworld, in which we 'always already' find ourselves as subjects capable of speaking and acting, can be reconciled with the contingency of the natural history of sociocultural forms of life. Hilary Putnam's internal realism provided me with impulses for a Kantian reading of pragmatism.[22] From this perspective, I return to ontological questions in the controversy with Quine, on the one hand, and with Heidegger, on the other. While nomological theories about domains of physically measurable objects rest on a 'nominalistic' linguistic ontology (in the medieval sense), the humanities and social sciences have to achieve their hermeneutic access to the object-domains of a symbolically structured lifeworld in concepts of a correspondingly 'realist' linguistic ontology. In the fifth introduction I will return to the question of whether and, if so, how this epistemic dualism can be reconciled with ontological monism.

3

Discourse Ethics

The anthology on the rehabilitation of practical philosophy edited by Manfred Riedel in 1974[1] provided confirmation of a reversal in trend that had taken place in the philosophy departments, a reversal that was also influenced by the student movement and was by no means confined to Germany. However, this book mirrors a curiously fractured landscape of various approaches. Whereas the essays on political philosophy reflect the neo-Aristotelian and Right-Hegelian reactions to the critical approaches of the 1960s, the contributions on moral philosophy by Karl-Otto Apel, Paul Lorenzen, Kuno Lorenz and myself are representative of the international trend towards replacing the predominance of empiricist approaches with theories that rehabilitated Kantian practical reason in the light of principles of universalization.

However, Germany lacked a counterpart to the deep caesura marked in the United States by the publication of John Rawls's *A Theory of Justice* in 1971. In Germany, the division of labour within the discipline was still so poorly developed that approaches in moral philosophy were part of more comprehensive projects such as the constructivism of the Erlanger school or Apel's transcendental pragmatics.[2] My case was no different in this respect. During the 1960s, I had dealt with the relationship between theory and practice initially in the context of social philosophy and the philosophy of history; these inquiries were situated in the area of intersection of practical philosophy and social theory and came into focus (for example, in the controversy with Karl Popper) in the specific problem of rational justification of decisions.[3] At the time, I encountered this problem, which is central for the theory of rationality, in different contexts: in the discussion on theories of technocracy,[4] in the methodological context of the problem of value judgements[5] and in the epistemological context of reason and interest.[6]

These discussions provided me with reasons to adopt complementary positions against scientism and decisionism, because the empiricist restriction of practical reason to instrumental rationality corresponds to the restriction of theoretical reason to a narrow, objectivist understanding of science. The abstract juxtaposition of 'decision' and 'cognition' is the result of a mistaken semantic abstraction of the propositional contents of knowledge from the pragmatic contexts of the problem-solving acquisition, communication and representation of these contents. However, *'reason' is inherently a matter of the use of reason.* Reasons are the medium of this use, and the discursive exchange of reasons still ensures – while allowing for all necessary differentiation between descriptive, evaluative and normative patterns of argumentation – a certain continuum that prevents the connection between theoretical and practical reason from being sundered completely. I did not conceive of moral philosophy as a 'free-standing' undertaking, but as a special part of the general theory of rational discourse. The task of a theory of morality is to explain how the validity claims raised for moral judgements can be redeemed. This approach proceeds via the theory of rationality and explains why I initially developed my version of 'discourse ethics', starting from the above-mentioned discussions of the 1960s, in the context of social theory. Facing the task of setting up a research programme at the Starnberg Institute in 1971–2, I had to come to terms with the issue of whether practical questions allow for truth or falsity at all. This was the philosophical question implied in the challenge of how to conceptualize the legitimacy of political regimes and how to evaluate the corresponding ideas that serve the function of political legitimation.[7]

Although we normally speak of 'legitimacy' only in the case of a political regime, the belief in its legitimacy has a moral core which is the same as that to be found in the mode of validity of any binding social norm. The starting point is the sociological observation that a normative order cannot be stabilized in the long run either by interlocking complementary interests or by mere threats of sanctions – interests can change, while sanctions cannot last forever. The maintenance of all normative orders also depends at least on a kind of unforced intersubjective recognition on the part of its addressees. Empirical motivations certainly play a role; but they alone cannot explain a permanent willingness of subjects to obey normatively binding behavioural expectations. The analysis of the obligatory character of norms of action that is prior to possible interests and sanctions had already made a Kantian out of Durkheim.[8] The deontic meaning of validity, whatever its genetic explanation, is based on the claim that a norm deserves recognition because it is 'right'. Addressees who accept such a claim believe (albeit in many cases counterfactually) that an existing norm (or an imperative justified in its light) regulates the behaviour of the persons concerned for the promotion of the 'common good' or 'in the equal interest of all'.

Whether it is based on illusion, habit, structural violence or rational motivation, this belief is no more immune to criticism than any other. However, whether norms are actually subjected to critical examination depends on contingent circumstances; one cannot tell simply by looking at accepted social norms whether they exist 'by right'. Ultimately, we can know this only about those norms that meet with the carefully considered agreement of all addressees under conditions of a rational discourse. It was this reflection that led me to a cognitivist interpretation of the contractualist idea of an 'original position', too. Every attempt to redeem normative validity claims recapitulates in a 'virtual' way the decisive reasons of the process of discursive will-information out of which the corresponding norms would have had to proceed in an imagined original position:

> Discourse can be understood as that form of communication that is removed from contexts of experience and action and whose structures assure us … that participants, themes, and contributions are not restricted …; that no force except that of the better argument is exercised; and that, as a result, all motives except that of the cooperative search for truth are excluded. If under these conditions a consensus about the recommendation to accept a norm arises argumentatively, that is, on the basis of hypothetically proposed, alternative justifications, then this consensus expresses a 'rational will'.[9]

This is not yet an answer to the central question as to why normative claims for recognition should have a cognitive meaning in the first place and could be redeemed with reasons. At that time, I was still content to appeal to the Kantian maxim that valid maxims must admit of being generalized: 'The discursively formed will may be called "rational" because the formal properties of discourse and of the deliberative situation sufficiently guarantee that a consensus can arise only through appropriately interpreted, *generalizable* interests, by which I mean *needs that can be communicatively shared*.'[10] At the time, I thought that a moral principle that would have to be justified in turn was unnecessary because 'the expectation of discursive redemption of normative validity claims is already contained in the structure of intersubjectivity that makes specially introduced maxims of universalization superfluous'.[11] This over-hasty conclusion of my first approach to moral cognitivism was mistaken about the burden of justification, a problem that I addressed only after the Starnberg period.

In the first part of this introduction, I will discuss five texts in which I developed discourse ethics. This theory of morality is intended to explain how moral validity claims can be redeemed; it also provides the key to analysing other normative validity claims, for example legal validity and political legitimacy. Discourse ethics has a narrower focus than traditional ethical theories because it concentrates on questions of justice as the questions that can be rationally decided in principle. Here it should be noted that the examination of normative validity claims in general refers to exactly one of three validity aspects of the more comprehensive reason embodied in use of language oriented to reaching an understanding and in communicative action (I). The reference to three further texts in the second part serves the purpose of classifying practical discourses. This section will deal, first, with the differentiation between the uses of practical reason, then address the relationship between normative validity, understood in epistemic terms, and the non-epistemic concept of truth and, finally, connect moral theory with the discourse theory of law and the democratic constitutional state to be dealt with in the fourth introduction (II).

I. Moral Theory

(1) During the 1960s, in a series of joint seminars conducted with Ulrich Oevermann on issues of socialization,

I had dealt with Jean Piaget's genetic structuralism and Lawrence Kohlberg's theory of moral development. But these theories first became relevant for my own work in connection with empirical research conducted at the Starnberg Institute (and through personal contacts with Kohlberg).[12] One result of the cooperation with Rainer Döbert and Gertrud Nunner-Winkler is the study on *Moral Consciousness and Communicative Action*, which I split off from the *Theory of Communicative Action*.[13] The philosophical point is a changed understanding of the relationship between morality and ethical life. The empirically demonstrated connection between the 'stages' of moral judgement and interactive competences shows that the postconventional form of consciousness conceptualized in terms of universalistic moral theories is not rooted in the ethical life of concrete historical forms of life, but instead in the basic features of linguistically structured forms of life in general. In more recent research, the tradition of genetic structuralism may have been forced into the background of such a highly specialized discipline as developmental psychology;[14] but it remains instructive as a guide for the *conceptual analysis* of the interconnections between moral consciousness and the competence of perspective-taking in communicative action.[15]

The differences between the versions of discourse ethics developed by Karl-Otto Apel and by me were grounded from the beginning in the contrast between a disciplinary and an interdisciplinary perspective on moral philosophy. While Apel regards the ultimate justification [*Letztbegründung*] of the moral principle as the royal road to the self-confirmation of philosophy, for me the task of justifying the moral principle arises in the context of a theory of communicative action that is tailored to the division of labour with other human sciences. In the present context, however, I refer to my first attempt to work out a moral theory in competition with other philosophical approaches in this field.[16]

My description of moral feelings following the work of Peter F. Strawson invites a cognitivist interpretation of the content of moral judgements against empiricist and value-sceptical conceptions.[17] And against a semantic analysis that takes its orientation from evaluative predicates like 'is good', I go on to emphasize the analogous illocutionary roles played by those expressions with which we raise assertoric and moral validity claims such as 'it is the case that p' and 'it is obligatory that h'. On the other hand, the conspicuous asymmetries between the use of declarative sentences and ought-statements are sufficient reason to emphasize, in contrast to realist conceptions of morality, the constructive character of the world of normatively regulated interpersonal relations.[18] My main concern is with the theme that obligatory norms are in need of recognition and the question of whether the corresponding normative validity claims can be redeemed with arguments – and, if so, how. The central thesis can be stated simply: those involved in moral-practical conflicts can achieve a consensual resolution even when they cannot rely on the support of a jointly recognized normative context. By engaging in a practical discourse, they tacitly accept certain demanding normative presuppositions of communication, so that the background understanding that Kant expresses in terms of the categorical imperative is generated performatively, that is, through mere participation in that practice of rational discourse.

Discourse ethics reformulates the intuition expressed in Kant's 'legislation formula' of the Categorical Imperative as a rule of argumentation in accordance with which 'all affected in their capacity as participants in a practical discourse' can proceed when they want to reach an agreement about controversial norms: 'Every valid norm has to fulfil the condition that *all* can accept the consequences and side effects its *general* observance can be anticipated to have for the satisfaction of *everyone's* interests (and these consequences are preferred to those of known alternative possibilities for regulation).'[19] This principle of universalization is one moral principle among many and is open to the suspicion that it expresses one-sided or culturally biased intuitions. Therefore, discourse ethics attempts to justify the universal validity of the principle by appealing to the idealizing content of the general and unavoidable presuppositions of argumentation. However, contrary to Apel's assumption, these presuppositions cannot be demonstrated [*bewiesen*] to be 'transcendentally necessary'. They can only be 'shown' [*aufgewiesen*], through an ad hoc rejection of performative contradictions, to be *non-rejectable* presuppositions of a practice to which there is no alternative because we do not know of any equivalent practices. Demonstrating this is sufficient to refute the objection of circularity which is often raised – namely, that the justification of the principle of universalization only extracts from the content of the presuppositions of argumentation what was already inserted into them *by definition*.

The 'justification' of the moral principle itself consists in proving that anyone who engages sincerely in a practical discourse, and hence accepts presuppositions of argumentation in general – and in addition knows what it means to justify a norm of action – already implicitly presupposes the validity of the principle of universalization. The line of thought can be expressed informally as follows: assuming that the practice of argumentation is based on the four essential presuppositions of (a) the inclusive and (b) equal participation of all affected, (c) the truthfulness of their utterances, and (d) the structurally guaranteed non-coerciveness of communication; then, in virtue of (a), (b) and (c), all relevant contributions can gain a hearing in practical discourses, but only those reasons can carry weight that accord equal consideration to everyone's interests and values; and in virtue of (c) and (d), only reasons of this kind (and not other motives) can be decisive for achieving agreement on a controversial norm.

(2) This justification step prompted persistent controversies not only on account of the incompleteness of the justification *programme*, but also because that first attempt indeed neglected two things: the *meaning of morality*, which is explained by the structural vulnerability of socialized individuals, and the fact that rational discourse, as a form of communication, not only accords the participants the communicative freedom to take stances when addressing practical questions, but also requires them to engage in *reciprocal perspective-taking*. Both of these moments are brought into focus when we trace moral judgement back to its lifeworld substrate and recognize that the communicative mode of socialization founds a *prior*, that is, genetic connection between moral questions and the form of communication in which practical discourses take place. Hegel's objections to Kant[20] alerted me to these gaps in my previous argument. The justification of the general validity of the principle of universalization also involves intuitive knowledge implicit in knowing how norms of action are justified, which in turn presupposes familiarity with the moral meaning of obligatory norms.

The need to justify norms of action arises only in situations in which the participants become explicitly aware of the difference between the mere fact of accepting a taken-for-granted 'ought' and the awareness that the validity claim of the corresponding norm is, for good reasons, worthy of being recognized. With this deontic dimension of the binding validity of norms that integrate the members of a collective into a network of reciprocal obligations, the meaning of morality becomes comprehensible as such. For socialized individuals, morality constitutes the protective mantle against the extreme and widespread intraspecific aggression characteristic of our species. *Homo sapiens* is especially vulnerable also because of its precarious and comparatively long period of socialization. Only creatures that are individuated in the course of their communicative socialization develop a functional imperative for something like 'morality'. They need a form of protection grounded in the precarious mode of socialization itself, because they can develop their personal identity only via the risky path of *externalizing* themselves *in social relations*. Therefore, the exposed and vulnerable integrity of the individual can be stabilized only in connection with the supportive social relations of mutual recognition. This meaning of morality finds expression in norms which *simultaneously* protect *both* the inviolability of the individual and the relations of reciprocal recognition as fellow members of a collective which reproduces itself, in turn, in the forms of legitimately regulated interpersonal relations.

The meaning of morality can be explained in terms of the answer to a challenge inherent in communicatively structured forms of life: people can stabilize their fragile identities *as individuals* only through *their membership* in an intersubjectively recognized normative order. Therefore, it is not surprising that the communicative shape of rational discourse, which is a kind of reflexive form of communicative action, is genetically related to this core of morality. Discourses allow the interest of each individual to come into play through the *freedom to say no*; but at the same time, they prevent the social bond from breaking by prompting the participants to *adopt each other's perspectives*. An agreement achieved by discursive means depends simultaneously on the 'yes' and 'no' responses of the participants and on their jointly overcoming their individual egocentrisms. This way of anchoring the moral point of view in the substrate of communicatively structured forms of life takes up Hegel's idea that morality is embedded in ethical life. However, this concession to Hegel in no way alters the Kantian formalism and cognitivism of a procedural conception of ethics. Morality refers to a need for protection that is explained by the communicative structure of our *form of life as such*. Discourse ethics limits itself to explaining only the moral point of view, with the reservation that the motivational bridge between moral judgements and action, i.e. the realization of moral relations, depends on 'accommodating' forms of life.

(3) An interview with my Danish colleague Torben Hviid Nielsen provided me with an opportunity to anticipate misunderstandings about the relationship between moral and social theory.[21] Whereas the sociologist adopts the third-person attitude of an observer, the moral theorist takes the participant perspective of someone who is involved and who, in moral conflicts, addresses her feelings and judgements in the first person to another, 'second' person. The fact that the questions of justice addressed by philosophy are not mere abstractions, but have a 'setting' in practical social life, in no way diminishes the independence of the analytical perspective of moral theory. The latter deals with genuinely philosophical questions, such as the rational decidability of moral disagreements, the role of moral feelings, the justification of moral principles, the explanation of the moral point of view, and so forth. As in other disciplines, every approach in moral theory has to be defended against competitors. On the other hand, we have to presuppose the validity of a particular moral theory when we make use of it in *other* contexts – for example, in sociology or psychology when we explain the social evolution of legal institutions or the development of moral forms of consciousness in children. But the field of application of theories of justice

is limited. For example, explanations of pathological social phenomena in terms of deformations of relations of recognition do not allow for any direct recourse to moral standards but require instead a clarified concept of communicative rationality in the light of which patterns of systematically distorted communication can be identified.[22]

For the rest, the interview is a *tour d'horizon* of objections that had been raised against discourse ethics. Among other things, it addresses the alleged Eurocentric bias of the deontological concept of justice, the distinction between traditional and modern societies, concepts such as 'performative contradiction' and 'ideal speech situation', the pluralism of the principles of justice, the relationship between morality and ethical life, the distinctions between discourses of justification and application, justice and solidarity, law and morality, and so forth. Also important for me is the role of moral feelings in a moral theory suspected of cold rationalism. At that time, virtue ethics, which today fills whole bookshelves, was not yet a topic of discussion. Otherwise I could have pointed out that the sober moral theory confined to explaining the moral point of view needs to be supplemented by an appealing moral *phenomenology*. For an eye-opening phenomenology, however, the literary skills and sensibilities of great philosophical writers, such as Nietzsche or Adorno or Levinas, are more suitable than the analytical abilities of conventional philosophers.

(4) In my essay 'Remarks on Discourse Ethics', I tried to clarify basic questions through a metacritical confrontation with competing theories – a kind of literature survey with systematic intent.[23] The contribution to my own theoretical approach resides more in the clarification of various details than in an improvement of the construction as a whole. An exception, however, is the important distinction between justification

and application discourses that I learned from Klaus Günther.[24] There is no need to add anything to the clear listing of the problems dealt with, except to refer to my subsequent discussion with John Rawls.[25] Even though by then I had got to know Rawls personally, at the time I had seriously digested only his *Theory of Justice* and was especially impressed by the article 'Kantian Constructivism'.[26] As yet, I had no knowledge of the series of intermediate steps that in the meantime had led Rawls, in view of the pressing phenomena of cultural pluralism, to make substantial revisions to his original conception in his draft for the soon-to-be-published book *Political Liberalism* (1993).[27]

What bothers me about Rawls's mature work is the decisive role he accords the doctrines of religious communities and ideological groups in contrast to the practical reason of the philosophers. He claims that there is an asymmetry between the public conceptions of justice, which can raise only a weak claim to 'reasonableness', and the religions and worldviews, to which he accords a strong claim to 'truth'.[28] The latter have the last word in the situation of overlapping consensus, and thus trump the secular proposals that appeal to practical reason alone. Although Rawls in his later work remains true to the general design of noncognitivist contract theories, the place of the self-interested citizens, who according to Hobbes make a rational choice in the transition from the state of nature to the social condition, is taken by the adherents of comprehensive doctrines who do not have to speak with one another, but only need to observe each other. All they need to establish is whether their views 'overlap' sufficiently that one of the liberal concepts of justice meets with agreement, even if each of them has different reasons for accepting them.

(5) Against the still widespread 'postmodern' misconception that moral universalism is a prescription for a kind of equal treatment that imposes uniformity

and inclusion through assimilation, I tried to show that
the decentring meaning of individualistic egalitarianism
provides the standard for a form of inclusion of others
in their otherness that is sensitive to difference.[29] The
moral community of all responsible persons is guided
by negative ideas on the abolition of discrimination, suf-
fering and marginalization. It thereby opens itself up for
the inclusion of strangers who want to remain strangers
to one another because it connects the justice of equal
individual freedoms with the joint involvement of fellow
subjects who stand in solidarity with each other, while
at the same time preserving the room for differences
of individual character and attitude. Like John Rawls,
therefore, I stylize religious and metaphysical pluralism
into the challenge to which postmetaphysical thinking
responds with different versions of a rational morality. From the historical point of view, I try to present
discourse ethics as the superior answer by comparison
with the main currents in modern moral philosophy,
an answer which, in the wake of the disintegration
of the supporting contexts of religion and metaphysics, renounces the shattered ethical background, but
replaces its substance with a normative procedural consensus that bridges all ideological differences. Discourse
ethics preserves the obligatory character of the moral
point of view, albeit at the cost of decoupling moral
principles from paths of salvation and thick ethical
models of life, by exploiting the only remaining shared
resource of the competing parties – namely, the communicative presuppositions of the discursive situation
of those who seek reasonable agreements in the face of
persistent practical conflicts.

In arguing thus, I adopt a different stance on religious
traditions from the late Rawls. On the one hand, I take
a more affirmative view of religion, because I see a close
genealogical connection between the Judeo-Christian
tradition and postmetaphysical rational morality. In

Europe, philosophy, insofar as it upholds an inclusive, individualistic and egalitarian conception of justice and solidarity, draws on the universalistic heritage of monotheism. On the other hand, I stress that the divine standpoint is transformed into a perspective that allows the human mind to regard the natural and social world *as a whole* from within the world. The moral point of view from which we can judge local conflicts impartially with reference to the totality of reasonably ordered interpersonal relations emerges from the transformation of the divine standpoint into inner-worldly transcendence. With this anthropocentric reversal of perspectives, practical reason claims a neutral place outside the battlefield of religions and worldviews and inverts the burden of justification in the conflict with the religions in its own favour. The genealogical connection between the legacy of world religions and rational morality cannot disguise the fact that, without the shift of epistemic authority from heaven to earth, the cognitive resource for secularizing the power of the state and taming it by rational means would have been lacking.

II. *On the System of Practical Discourses*

Discourse theory separates questions of justice from ethical questions – that is, from questions of the good life, of how to live one's life and what is the best for us to do. Because it concentrates on explaining sharply defined moral claims to validity, the name that has become established for this position, 'discourse *ethics*', is not quite correct. In the second part of this introduction I refer to texts that go beyond the domain of moral theory in this narrower sense. These texts compare the moral with the ethical and pragmatic uses of practical reason (6), address the epistemological question of the distinction between the truth of statements and the deontic validity of norms (7) and, finally, broaden our view of the entire discursive landscape of morality, law and politics (8).

(6) Kant understood freedom in general as the ability of a subject to bind her will to maxims. His distinction between the freedom of choice of purposive-rational actors and the free will of morally acting subjects draws attention to different constellations of the will and practical reason. I supplement Kant's taxonomy of the uses of practical reason with a third element.[30] Between the purposive-rational choice of means and the value-oriented weighing of ends, on the one hand, and moral judgement and action, on the other, is situated the ethical self-understanding of a person about what she really wants and should want, and ultimately about *who she is and would like to be*. To be sure, in each case 'freedom' in the sense of self-obligation is at work. But the pragmatic, ethical and moral uses of reason differ not only as regards the type of practical reasons involved, but also in how far the rational weighing of practical reasons *permeates and binds* the faculty of will, as it were. When we make a pragmatic use of our practical reason, the values and ends that we desire (or assume as already given) remain, as contingent 'motivations' [*Beweggründe*], beyond the scope of argumentation. When it is a matter of forming an ethical-existential self-understanding, by contrast, value orientations are the actual theme, so that here both reason and the will mutually condition each other. It is only when the subject acts in accordance with laws that she has given herself from moral insight that the will is *completely permeated* and determined by practical reason – and eradicates the last trace of heteronomy. Here the free will is not bound by anything 'given' – neither by prior values or preferences, nor by a life history awaiting critical appropriation.

The intersubjectivist character of deontological morality enables us to make a clear distinction between

the *egocentric perspective* from which we generalize
maxims, yielding the Golden Rule, and the *decentred
standpoint of the first-person plural* in terms of which
all affected interests can be discussed and accorded
equal consideration. Only under the condition of mutual
perspective-taking can participants in an inclusive discourse take into account the diversity of interests of all
of those concerned. In addition, the intersubjectivist
reading alerts us to the fact that practical discourses
can be legally institutionalized, for example in courts
or parliaments. Given the different possible uses of
practical reason, finally, the question of the unity of
practical reason arises. At this point, we must not make
the mistake of calling for a metadiscourse that would
control the transition from one discourse to the other
as it were 'from above', from the point of view of a
philosopher king. The progressive inclusion of different
kinds of practical questions must not be confused with a
'natural' hierarchy among the corresponding pragmatic,
ethical, moral or legal discourses. If existing preferences
become problematic, then it is advisable to move from
pragmatic to ethical discourses, and if one person's life
project violates the legitimate expectations of others,
then the transition from ethical to moral discourse suggests itself. But if a dispute breaks out over whether a
problematic situation whose import remains unclear
'should' be treated from the moral point of view at all,
and not, instead, from points of view of expediency or
of which of the competing goods is preferable, then
there is no metadiscourse that can claim the authority
to resolve this dispute. On the other hand, falling back
on a pre-discursive faculty of judgement that performs
this function as it were 'from below' is not an option
either. We therefore have to place our trust in the power
of *the problems themselves* to push for differentiations,
to sort out the appropriate patterns of argumentation
and to *prompt* the parties to engage in the right form of

discourse. This conception is plausible, of course, only within a communicative paradigm that understands the self-referential operations of the human mind as movements within the intersubjective space of reasons.

(7) There remains the difficult question that every cognitivist theory of morality faces: in what sense can we associate with moral judgements a claim to rightness analogous to the claim to truth of assertoric statements? This question has been addressed traditionally in the context of the relationship between theoretical and practical reason. But the problem is better understood in terms of a relationship between the corresponding claims to validity. If we want to speak of moral 'truths' in an *analogous* sense to the truth of declarative statements, then we must distinguish between the similarities and the differences in the procedures of justifying one and the other. A strong motivation for *comparing* moral with assertoric validity claims is in the first place that we do not think it pointless to engage in reasoned argumentation about moral utterances. They cannot be *equated*, however, because moral validity claims lack the ontological connotation of reference to a world of objects *existing independently of our descriptions of them*. The ontic meaning of the 'existence of states of affairs' stands in contrast to the deontological meaning of moral precepts that demand respect and require actors to do or refrain from doing something. Whereas we find and encounter the objective world of which we can have knowledge, it is we who first give rise to the social world of interpersonal relationships, which we can judge from the moral point of view. *Moral judgements and practical discourses are themselves part of that ongoing constructive activity.*

It is not pointless to raise the question of the relationship between 'construction' and 'discovery' with regard to the theoretical use of reason either, though in this case the constructive anticipation serves the purpose of comprehending a state of affairs, whereas practical knowledge directs action.[31] The *terminus a quo* and the *terminus ad quem* are reversed in these two cases. Whereas the free will binds itself in the practical use of reason, the theoretical use of reason does not have any impact on the constellation of reason and the will. Therefore, the description of discourse ethics as 'cognitivist' should not be misinterpreted as a version of moral realism. Although there are no moral facts independent of our moral practices, moral judgements and norms can nevertheless be judged to be right or wrong because the 'social world' imposes restrictions on them, albeit in a different sense to the restrictions that the objective world places on statements that can be true or false. Of course, the social contexts in which we actually find ourselves can hardly be constitutive of such restrictions, because existing norms in turn face the critical question of whether they also deserve the social recognition of their addressees.

A first indication of the alleged restriction placed on our moral judgements by the infrastructure of the social world of interpersonal relations is provided by the principle of universalization. According to this principle, only those moral judgements and norms are valid that could be accepted for good reasons by all those affected giving equal consideration to the relevant claims of each of them. It is this constructive perspective of the equal inclusion of others in an inclusive world of agreed-upon norms which, in the case of moral judgements, takes the place of the justification-transcendent reference of assertoric statements to the objective world. This reference point of an idealized social world of relations among free and equal persons explains the epistemic character of the justification-immanent meaning of moral rightness. But there are many ideals. Therefore, it must first be shown that the individualistic-egalitarian design of such an ideal world of legitimately ordered interpersonal relations is not one among many, but is deeply rooted in the communicative constitution of all sociocultural forms of life.

This is why I tried to demonstrate the plausibility of the analogy between rightness and truth[32] by arguing that there is an internal connection between our version of the 'kingdom of ends' and the communicative presuppositions of practical discourse. For this purpose, I use the evolutionary argument that there is an increasing convergence between the diversity of historical concepts of justice and the discursive procedure of judging moral-practical conflicts. The idea of justice, which first assumes the form of concrete conceptions in the particularistic contexts of tribal societies and early civilizations, progressively loses its substantive content with increasing social complexity, until finally the propositional content of 'justice' withdraws into the procedural form of *impartial judgement*. The scenario of the disintegration of the communal forms of ethos and the increasing pluralism of forms of life and worldviews explains why the substantive ideas of justice, in terms of which the worthiness of moral principles and of norms to be recognized is measured, finally dissolve into the idea of discursive procedural justice. The semantic content of *justice* converges with a procedural notion of *impartiality* that is operationalized in the form of an agreement achieved in rational discourse.

This convergence can be explained by the fact that, in the case of moral judgement, the communicative presuppositions of argumentation refer not only to the semantic level of the mobilization of contents or to the pragmatic level of the exchange of arguments, but also to *the character of the participants themselves*. In fact, when it comes to practical questions, the presuppositions of argumentation not only imply that the requisite semantic contents (relevant topics and contributions, reliable information and reasons) are brought into play and that the better arguments tip the scales. Because practical discourse, as a form of communication, and the meaning of the moral question are rooted in the same communicative mode of socialization, here the pragmatic presuppositions of discourse that depend on the goodwill of the participants – the truthfulness of one's own utterances and the equal consideration accorded those of other persons – acquire a direct practical meaning: they enjoin the participants, when articulating a shared interpretation of values and needs, to express themselves authentically and to *perform the act of empathy* that is required for what George Herbert Mead describes as *reciprocally adopting* the *perspectives* of the others involved. Practical discourses are essentially a matter of the participants working to overcome these differences in perspective.

Conflicts of action are sparked by the resistance of opponents with conflicting value orientations. From the moral point of view, such conflicts are transformed into problems and the corresponding forms of resistance into as many objections of participants in discourse. Therefore, the correct resolution of a pending problem consists in the convincing reasons for an appropriate – i.e., *sufficiently inclusive* – enlargement of the shared perspective from which the participants interpret and evaluate the problem. 'Rightness', unlike 'truth', is an epistemic validity claim – i.e., one immanent to justification – because in moral questions, discursively achieved agreement *is synonymous with* developing a sufficiently inclusive enlargement of the jointly adopted perspective for both interpretation and evaluation. At the end of the essay in question, I touch on the speculative issue of whether, historically speaking, a higher-level 'ethical judgement' is needed to transfer the binary code of 'true' and 'false' to practical questions. For it is this transfer that first constitutes the subset of discursively answerable moral questions of justice. This consideration creates the prospect of a 'species ethics', which I have addressed in other contexts.[33]

(8) Karl-Otto Apel and I initially developed the discourse-ethical approach in cooperation. It would seem appropriate, therefore, to explain the disagreements that have arisen, especially since my attempt to make this approach fruitful for the philosophy of law.[34] But here I can only refer the reader to an attempt to specify the place in the system of practical discourses where juridical and moral discourses diverge because of the more complex structure of legal norms. I recommend this brief reply to a much more extensive critique by Apel[35] because it offers an account of the relationship between the discourse theories of truth, morality and law, while at the same time providing an introduction to the normative principles of political theory.

4

Political Theory

Although the classical works of political philosophy – from Aristotle through Hobbes to Rousseau and Kant – are still our contemporaries, political theories remain tied especially closely to their context of origin. I would therefore like to offer a few preliminary remarks about the situation of my generation after the caesura in world history of 1945. It was impossible for us *not* to take a stance, be it defensive or self-critical, on the revelations about the crimes committed by the Nazi regime. Although it was only after completing my studies that I began to deal with questions of politics in a broader sense – namely, with Marxist social theory, constitutional law and political sociology – the political confrontation with the fact that our population broadly supported the Nazi regime remains for us more than just one topic among others up to the present day.

'Democracy in Germany' was therefore the yardstick against which we also measured the politics of the day. The political culture of the early Federal Republic was marked by a gulf between fragile democratic institutions and barely disrupted authoritarian mentalities. In academia, as in almost all functional domains, there was an unbroken continuity at the level of personnel. The intellectual trailblazers of the old regime, with a few exceptions, had survived the denazification process unscathed. They felt safe from criticism and saw no reason for self-criticism. The continuities in personnel and mentalities that persisted behind the cloak of anti-communism kept the fear of a relapse into the authoritarian behavioural patterns and elitist habits of thought of pre-democratic Germany alive – in my case even into the early 1980s.

The anti-anti-communism that we opposed to the disturbing profile of the Adenauer era was accused of 'totalitarian' thinking by the other side. The dispute over mentalities in the Federal Republic led to a polarization in the course of the student movement not only in the universities, a polarization that continues to exert effects to the present day in the controversies over the legacy of '1968'. Even while engaged in this melee, I tried to separate the role of the intellectual as clearly as possible from that of the scholar and the academic teacher. The way in which the corresponding texts were presented was also intended to clarify this distinction. However, it is not always easy to sort publications into academic treatises, on the one hand, and 'short political writings' [*Kleine politische Schriften*], on the other.[1]

Political judgements are shaped, although not necessarily prejudiced, by the contexts in which they emerge. The dissent triggered by critical experiences can mobilize good reasons. The *nationalist, authoritarian and voluntaristic* features of the Nazi regime embodied a political pathology from which something could be learnt. If we assume that the holders of political power are authorized to make collectively binding decisions, three questions arise: How is the collectivity for which the rulers make political choices defined? Who has access to political power and is authorized to make binding decisions? How is the medium of the exercise of political power itself conceived? To these questions Nazi ideology provided the fatally wrong answers 'nation and destiny', 'the party and the leader' and 'decision and self-assertion', respectively.

The *nationalist* conception of the 'Volk' ignores not only the cultural and ideological heterogeneity of the population and the individualism of the democratic constitution, but also more generally the complexity of a functionally differentiated *society*. The rule embodied by the *authoritarian* leader has to orchestrate the acclamation of the masses and to respond to oppositional voices with repression, because it substitutes the will of a state party for the polyphonic stances of its citizens. It has to compensate for the deficiency of spontaneous legitimation with violence. Finally, the *voluntaristic* confusion of the exercise of political power with existential self-assertion that is ready to resort to violence misses the cognitive dimension of the medium of power. Legitimate power is communicatively generated and administratively exercised in order to mobilize resources for pursuing collective goals. Political action shares features of partisanship not because it is essentially a matter of decision, but because collective decisions subject to the risk of error reach into an uncertain future.

The ineradicable element of decision in collective action under conditions of uncertainty is merely the reverse side of the fallibility of the high expectations of rationality that go hand in hand with the pursuit of collective goals. What sets political action apart at all stages of the development, determination and implementation of collectively binding programmes is the *internal connection between taking stances and solving problems*. This connection is taken into account by *inclusion and deliberation* as the two essential features of democratic politics. The democratic procedure is designed to unleash the communicative liberties of *all* citizens and to transform their partisanship under conditions of discursive opinion and will-formation into productive forces for the legitimate – i.e., *simultaneously interest-generalizing and effective* – influence that a politically organized society exercises over itself.

If one views fascism through the lens of a pathologist, then the discursive formation of political will by the citizens presents itself as a suitable therapeutic goal – and simultaneously as a means for democratizing a political culture that at the time remained mired in authoritarian mentalities. This also explains my theoretical interest in the design and structural transformation of the public sphere.[2] In contrast to the nationalistic picture of a political community integrated through a *Volk*, this perspective reveals the complex interconnections between the state and civil society, on the one hand, and functionally differentiated subsystems, on the other. Moreover, the patterns of political mass communication provide a basis for comparing the conditions of legitimation of authoritarian and democratic forms of domination. Finally, the communicative liquefaction of political will-formation reveals something of the rationalizing dynamic that can also transform the substance of political power itself in the long run. The opaque core of pre-democratic state power, which even democratic states maintain against internal and external 'enemies', can be dissolved in the medium of public discourses.

Prior to any theoretical interest, the crux of democracy for me was, apart from the political participation of the citizens, the deliberative mode of rational political will-formation. The research climate in Germany in which I attempted to clarify this issue was shaped by four *intellectual currents*: Critical Social Theory, which I assimilated at the Institute for Social Research in Frankfurt; a theory of constitutional law, advocated by Carl Schmitt and his students, which brings a substantive conception of the state into opposition to pluralistic society; the technocratic description of the state in industrial society developed by Freyer, Gehlen and

Schelsky; and, finally, Joachim Ritter's neo-Aristotelian interpretation of Hegel's philosophy of right, which would inspire the work of the 'Münster School'.

Critical Theory sharpened my awareness of the precarious connection between democracy, the state and the economy. The orientation to the public interest of the constitutional state, which guarantees its citizens equal liberties, communication and participation rights and social rights, is inherently in tension with the imperatives of a market economy which limit the scope for action of the tax-financed state apparatus. While the state itself has been differentiated into one functional subsystem alongside others, the political community must keep communication and decision-making channels open through a public sphere anchored in civil society, and thereby ensure that society *as a whole* can exercise democratic influence over itself. Thus, the normative meaning embodied in democratic practices inevitably clashes with the inertia, complexity and recalcitrance of a functionally differentiated society.

The question of how 'facticity' and 'validity' contend with each other explains why I conceive of political theory as part of a *reconstructive*, and only to this extent normative, theory of society – and not as a purely philosophical construction of the 'well-ordered' society or as merely empirical political sociology.[3] The older Critical Theory is so profoundly shaped by the historical experiences of fascism and Stalinism that it understands political rule as totalitarian in principle. The *Dialectic of the Enlightenment* is also a theory of totalitarianism. The reformist educational programme practised by Horkheimer and Adorno after the Second World War did not find a systematic place within Critical Theory itself. At the time, I was interested in the interventionist state's scope for exercising democratic influence over the capitalist economy. Keynesianism was in the air[4] and I had always been sceptical about a functionalist version of Marxism for which the rule of law and democracy are merely dependent variables.

Spiros Simitis drew my attention to the famous controversies between the leading constitutional lawyers during the Weimar period. Among those legal experts, it was Carl Schmitt, ironically enough, who left behind the most controversial but also the most influential traces in the post-war period. His disciples had adapted to the new conditions in the manner of a 'reluctant modernism' and were up to date with developments in the discussion.[5] The Schmittian school thematized the relationship between the state, the economy and society along the anti-liberal lines of Right Hegelianism. In this reading, the political public sphere is treated as the forum over which the dissonant cacophony of interest groups and political parties gains pre-parliamentary and extra-parliamentary influence, thereby undermining the positivity of the unified will of the state. This invocation of the 'substance' of the power of the state against the fragmenting and dissolving tendencies of a self-organizing society played for me the role of an instructive counter-model to a theory of democracy nourished by the spirit of deliberative politics.

A certain tendency to idealize the origins of bourgeois democracy in *Structural Transformation of the Public Sphere* can also be explained by the 'motif of rationalizing the exercise of social and political authority through publicity'.[6] What I lacked at the time was not so much historical examples as the conceptual tools of discourse theory to develop a clear normative concept of deliberative politics based on the empirical material. But the controversy with two other representatives of reluctant modernism made it clear to me how the dissolution of the violence at the core of political power through rational discourse must *not* be conceived.

Arnold Gehlen's slogan that the functional systems of society, namely the state, the economy, science and technology, were 'ultra-stable' was intended to point to a 'crystalline condition' of *posthistoire*. His approach was a very German variant of the theory of technocracy also in vogue at the time in the United States and France. This reading derives its antidemocratic edge from the assumption that the 'objective laws' of the functionally differentiated and mutually stabilizing subsystems leave no room for superfluous political deliberations over practical questions.[7] This theory can be understood as an anthropologically based forerunner of system functionalism; however, it lacks the basic conceptual clarification of the relationship between systemic and purposive rationality that Niklas Luhmann would provide.[8] In contrast to the auratic decisionism of the Schmittians, Gehlen and Schelsky developed the disenchanted picture of a political administration that is largely freed from the need to make decisions by following functional imperatives, and thus no longer needs democracy even as a backdrop for mass acclamation.[9]

The Aristotelian distinction between *praxis* and *techne*, and thus the moral-practical logic of political action geared to balancing interests, could be cited against the simplifications of both sides. On the other hand, the recourse to Aristotle is weighed down by the legacy of a pre-modern concept of politics that represents the political community as the centre of society *as a whole*. With a dichotomous picture of state and society, therefore, Joachim Ritter appealed to a differentiated reading of Hegel's philosophy of right. According to Ritter, 'civil' society that has developed into 'industrial' society detaches itself as a structurally autonomous natural basis from the historical horizon of the lifeworld, while the legal persons who are protected in their private autonomy are released into the domain of subjective liberties freed from the constraints of social organization.

This conception has the advantage of taking the achievements of the constitutional state seriously.

However, it limits the protected sphere of a historically shaped culture to the defensive role of absorbing the shock waves of social change generated by a self-propelling technological progress. Culture merely compensates for the costs of social modernization and nourishes a civic practice interpreted in neo-Aristotelian terms that depends essentially on the 'supporting powers', that is, on the hermeneutic appropriation of religious and national traditions. Furthermore, the Aristotelian conceptions of *praxis* and *phronesis* are too weak to invest political discourse with the energy to rationalize the arbitrary core of political power. My studies in the history of philosophy on the relationship between theory and practice already revolved around the question of how to understand the rational core of political practice. My tentative reflections on the scientization of political practice inspired by Dewey's *The Quest for Certainty* did not take me much farther either.[10] Only the approach of discourse ethics did justice to the interest-*generalizing*, and in general the cognitive dimension, and pointed to a discourse theory of law and constitutional democracy.

I began work on this project in 1986 with the Tanner Lectures[11] and I completed it over the following five years in cooperation with an interdisciplinary working group on the theory of law.[12] After completing *Between Facts and Norms*, I dealt, on the one hand, with different aspects of the connections between democracy, the rule of law and political culture as they appear within the framework of the national state (I–III) and, on the other, with the challenges faced by the nation-state in the postnational constellation (IV).[13]

I. Democracy

(1) For the impending bicentennial of the French Revolution, I delivered a lecture that recalls the

revolutionary beginnings of republican democracy and reflects the ambivalent academic echo that this date had triggered, especially in France, among former communist historians.[14] Quite apart from the occasion, there are good reasons to ask whether the traces of the original revolutionary mindset have been effaced entirely in the normalized constitutional democracies of the present day, or whether the embers of the intellectual origins still glow to some degree in every democratic order capable of withstanding crises – specifically, the recollection of the break with obsolete traditions, the courage to embrace new beginnings and the willingness to take a reflexive stance on cultural certainties and habitual practices. Democracy is associated with the idea that citizens should take their destinies into their own hands not only as individuals; rather, they are also called upon to become authors of their social and political destiny in their role as participants in a shared practice of opinion- and will-formation. If this idea is to find (and maintain) an echo in reality under conditions of social complexity, then it must shape the institutions of the constitutional state and the practices of its citizens.

However, the ground on which these institutions are built is constantly shifting. If the citizens are to lend their convictions and interests public force, they must make a vital use of their anarchic communicative liberties. On the other hand, a population will exercise its rights all the more readily the more it is accustomed to democratic liberties. The democratic constitutional state depends on motivations oriented to the public interest that cannot be legally enforced, however modest their scale may be. The capitalist dynamics of that highly productive economic society whose mobilizing power is celebrated by Marx and Engels in the *Communist Manifesto* must therefore find a counteracting complement in the cultural dynamics of civil society. Otherwise, the politically untamed dynamic of 'creative destruction' (Schumpeter) will break the overstrained bond of civic solidarity which can in any case be maintained only in an abstract form.

The citizens can avoid entrusting their collective fate to the centrifugal forces of a self-regulating system operating above their heads only as long as the democratic idea of an association of free and equal individuals who give themselves laws retains the utopian spark that can at any time spring from the ashes of daily routines and burst into the flames of an emphatic defence of violated rights. How can this idea of national sovereignty maintain a setting in the life of functionally differentiated societies that are becoming more and more complex with every passing day? In the above-mentioned lecture, I present three conceptual orientations that I went on to develop in chapters 7 and 8 of *Between Facts and Norms*.

Classical republicanism is still wedded to the fiction that the people is the embodiment of sovereign power. The communication-theoretical approach translates this concretistic reading into procedures and forms of communication of deliberative politics which justify the assumption that the resulting decisions are rationally motivated and point to learning processes. The 'body politic', the 'self' of self-government, becomes dispersed in legitimizing discourses and decision-making competences. The sovereign will of the people dissolves into a complex of circuits of communication, although the chain of legitimation, comprising a variety of links of opinion- and will-formation, must of course remain *anchored* in the electoral decisions of the citizens.

A stumbling block along the path to translating 'popular sovereignty' into a theory of communication is the differentiation of the state apparatus into a functionally specified subsystem of a decentralized society so that the polity is no longer 'pinnacle or centre' (Luhmann) of society but forms only one among many of its parts. This is reflected in the distinction between the communicative power of the citizens and the administrative power of the state apparatus. The citizens generate communicative power in the currency of 'relevant topics' and 'good reasons' by influencing the agendas of the state institutions through the formation of public opinion and through electoral decisions; the administrative power employed by the state to implement political programmes derives its legitimacy in turn from this source. The threshold at which communicative is transposed into administrative power calls to mind the indirect way in which society exercises democratic influence over itself.

At the same time, 'the people', even if it does not govern itself, does not simply allow the government to rule 'in its name'. A public sphere that is receptive to communicative inputs from civil society constitutes the link between the institutions of the state and the sounding-board of a lifeworld that is in turn responsive to the external costs of the functional disruptions requiring political regulation. From a historical point of view, however, the political parties, which are the most influential actors in the mass media public sphere, have in a sense changed sides: spokespersons and representatives of civil society have mutated into unofficial organs of state. Thus, it is an empirical question *how* the organization of mass loyalty as it were from above *interpenetrates* with the opposing process of the spontaneous opinion- and will-formation springing from the cells of civil society. The vitality, the perceptiveness and the level of the public discourses depend to a large extent on the semantic potential, the depth and the articulatory power of a political culture that shapes a population's imagination and sense of justice.

If we make the procedural conception of deliberative politics central to the theory of democracy, then differences from both the republican and liberal traditions become apparent. The deliberative model has been a comparatively weak voice in the history of political ideas; in juxtaposing the three normative models of democracy, therefore, I am less interested in a historical comparison than in making a systematic comparison intended to sharpen the profiles of the three models.[15] The three theoretical approaches develop quite different notions of the state and society and of the political process. Because discourse theory does not make realizing deliberative politics contingent on a citizenry capable of collective action but instead on forms of communication and on institutionalized procedures, it forges a connection between the participant's view and the objectifying perspective of the scientific observer on the democratic process. But it does not throw the baby out with the bathwater by replacing the expectations of virtue with which the republican doctrine weighs down political decision-making with the liberal game of an aggregation of individual interests. Rather, with everyday communication, it offers a pre-political source of 'solidarity' that is relevant for the political consciousness of the citizens and that, as a medium through which society as a whole is integrated, serves as a counterbalance to the other two media of integration, the 'market' and 'political power'.

This theoretical comparison raises the question of how the deliberative model can be coupled with empirical research. I addressed this question in 2006 in a lecture delivered at the World Congress of the International Association for Media and Communication Research.[16] Social-psychological studies on small groups can test the rational potential ascribed to political deliberation directly. By contrast, political science deals with large-scale communication processes. If popular sovereignty withdraws into the procedure of democratic will-formation and the legal implementation of its more or less demanding forms of communication, then the relevant empirical investigations must refer to the functions that the circuits of political communication have to fulfil if they are to exercise legitimizing effects *as a whole*, *in different* arenas and *at different* levels – specifically, in civil society, in the public sphere and in state institutions. Many empirical objections against the concept of deliberative politics are groundless because they start from an insufficiently complex picture of the legitimation process.

An example is the picture of a discourse among those present, which ideally fulfils various functions simultaneously. Such a discourse should mobilize relevant topics, necessary information and appropriate contributions; it should promote alternative stances on opposing positions and make it possible to evaluate them in the light of good reasons; and, finally, it should allow only rationally motivated decisions to influence procedurally correct decisions. With a view to a large-scale legitimation process, it is indispensable as a preliminary conceptual matter to assign these different functions to different forms and arenas of communication and, if necessary (as in the case of the administration of justice), even to special types of discourse. The aforementioned lecture refers mainly to the informal contribution of mass communication to the legitimation process among the broad public. From a normative perspective, this process can be restricted to filtering socially relevant issues and controversial positions, the requisite information and suitable arguments out of the inputs of civil society, of politics and from the representatives of the functional subsystems and processing them into 'published' opinions. When these are weighed up in turn in the light of the stances of the public, they can give rise to more or less reflected 'public' opinions. Post-democratic conditions can be plainly seen from the conspicuous symptoms of the disintegration of these complex structures of publicity (for example, in the case of populist referendums that 'go off the rails').

II. *The Constitutional State*

The disciplinary separation between political and legal theory, between political science and jurisprudence, should not obscure the fact that there is an internal – i.e. conceptual – connection between law and political power. The amalgam of coercive force and normative validity claim that we observe in the medium of state law dates back to the historical origins of state-organized power in the early civilizations. The tension between facticity and validity is manifested in inverse form in the two components of political power and law: political domination, which has control over means of sanction, is authorized by legitimate law, while the law that generates legitimate validity is sanctioned and implemented by state power.[17] In the ancient empires, of course, the imperial link between politics and law was still based on the legitimating force of 'strong' traditions that appeal to God or to a cosmic order and lend credibility to a source of *authority beyond society*. It is only with the positivization of law and the concentration of power in the modern state apparatus, with its monopoly on the use of force, that the metasocial authority of worldviews becomes incorporated in society itself – henceforth society must produce its own legitimations. The two eighteenth-century constitutional revolutions provide different answers to this challenge, which nevertheless converge in making a connection between democracy and the rule of law justified by appeal to natural rights theories.

Once the sovereign ruler has become a political legislator, the same question arises for the legitimacy of law and for the legitimacy of political power: how can the power of the political legislator and the legal order to which it gives rise claim legitimacy if both are based on nothing other than the positivity of the arbitrary will of a sovereign – irrespective of whether sovereign power is embodied in the prince, a plurality of representatives or the people? The question is not much different when the sovereign is still operating within the framework of the *continuation* of a legal system which, like that of common law, ultimately rests on the mere facticity of adjudication, custom and habit. I take as my starting point the formal characteristics of positive law and the complementary relation between law and morality and find the answer to the question of the *emergence of legitimacy from legality* in the democratic procedure and its legal institutionalization.[18] Democratic opinion- and will-formation must satisfy two conditions: all those affected must be included in the decision-making process, and the deliberations leading up to the decisions must fulfil certain deliberative standards.[19] This requires in turn that the procedure in question must be legally institutionalized; the constitutional state must make use of the legal medium to enable both inclusive participation and discursive opinion- and will-formation by the people.

Of course, the political participation and communication rights and the complex network of legitimizing discourses only secure the *public* autonomy of the citizens. Under the contingent conditions of life in modern societies, however, they can make appropriate use of their public autonomy only if a uniform and materially assured *private* autonomy ensures that they are sufficiently independent. This dialectical relationship between private and public autonomy is the key to solving the problem of how to reconcile the two legitimating pillars on which the constitutional state rests. I developed the question of the competition versus the compatibility of 'popular sovereignty' and the 'rule of law' in detail in chapter 3 of *Between Facts and Norms*, and took it up once again in the context of the long-running American discussion of the legitimacy of constitutional judicial review.[20] Radical democrats have to come to grips with the liberal principle that *democracy cannot define democracy*. This principle is contradicted by the democratic legitimacy that the constitution-building process claims for itself.[21] Rather than taking refuge in the usual paradoxes at this point, I ground the *co-originality of democracy and the rule of law* by arguing that constitutional law can guarantee the political empowerment of *democratic citizens* only simultaneously with the private autonomy of these same persons in their role as *private citizens*. In the debate with Frank Michelman, I explicate this thesis once again in terms of a conceptual reconstruction of the necessary reasons that first qualify a practice as one of constitution-building. This conceptual-genealogical view enables me, in addition, to develop a dynamic understanding of the democratic constitution. Each following generation can call to mind the performative meaning of founding a constitution – namely, to create a voluntary association of free and equal citizens by means of positive law, specifically through the reciprocal recognition of basic rights. This intuitive meaning of an exemplary practice is made explicit in constitutional documents, and it can serve for following generations as a standard for relating in a critical spirit, under changed historical conditions and in the light of new challenges, to the text of the constitution with the intention of arriving at a *successively more exhaustive specification* of the existing system of rights.

III. Nation, Culture and Religion

If the reproduction of liberal institutions depends ultimately on the citizens' correct use of their communicative freedoms, then the political culture of a population educated to freedom and accustomed to political freedom plays an important role in this conception of democracy. However, this should not be understood as implying that the constitutional state can justify itself towards its citizens only by appeal to 'pre-political sources' such as the nation or religion. Constitutional principles can be justified *only by using the sober means of postmetaphysical thinking* as a basis for legitimizing a fully secularized and *completely* juridified exercise of political rule. On the other hand, these judicious principles must also put down roots in the beliefs and mentalities of the citizens if reasons are to become practical motivations. The democratic state must expect its citizens in their role as co-legislators to exhibit a certain degree of orientation to the common good, even if it cannot and must not legally enforce such motives. This brings into play the liberal spirit of a political culture that diverts energies from 'pre-political' sources, *filters* them and directs them into the channels of a *civic ethos* to provide the citizens with guidance in the correct use of their communicative freedoms.[22]

This filtering function becomes clear once we clarify the relationship between the nation and the constitutional state. Pre-political sources, such as a shared religious background, the common language and above all the easily inflamed national consciousness, were indeed helpful from a historical point of view when it came to filling the empty legal forms of abstract civic solidarity with motivation. But when these traditional powers seize *direct* control over the legal culture by creating the appearance of a second nature, then the boundaries between ethnos and demos become blurred. And every form of ethnocentrism erodes the universalistic meaning of democratic citizenship.

Following the collapse of the Soviet Union, certain political developments in Eastern Europe provided me with an occasion to clarify the concepts of 'nation of citizens' [*Staatsbürgernation*] and 'ethnic nation' [*Volksnation*].[23] Meanwhile, migration flows are now also giving rise to nationalist movements in West European countries as the latter undergo the painful process of transformation into postcolonial immigrant societies. Growing cultural and ideological pluralism is triggering struggles over recognition aimed at the inclusion of the minorities in ways that are sensitive to difference. In those first-generation nation-states, the political culture had become fused with indigenous majority cultures in ways which were taken for granted. This amalgam turns the differentiation of a political culture that includes all citizens equally and crystallizes around the universalist core of the constitution into a protracted process. The concept of the nation of citizens plays an important role not only when it comes to issues of multiculturalism but also when faced with quests for national self-determination or with conflicts over the future of the European Union.

However, this concept is in need of defence not only against fundamentalist opposition, be it nationalist or religious in origin. The more serious criticism is the one aimed at the egalitarian-universalist foundations of abstract law and democracy itself.[24] A postmodern version of liberalism tries to deconstruct the idea of equality with objections grounded in the critique of reason. According to this view, the notion of equal freedoms is paradoxical because the legitimate claims of the very life projects of individuals that are supposed to be accorded equal consideration are inevitably violated by an impartial application of general norms. On closer inspection, it is argued, the practice of treating different cases, persons or life histories equally reveals the violence actually inflicted on the incomparable individuality of the individual by the abstract universality of norms. This mistaken reading is based on a confusion of the perspective of a first person who is concerned about his or her own life with the we-perspective of citizens who, in their role as democratic fellow legislators, jointly prescribe for themselves the norms in accordance with which they want to regulate their social life. It is only from this participant perspective, which overcomes the egocentrism of the first person through reciprocal perspective-taking, that questions of justice can even be posed.

Equally groundless are the doubts expressed by proponents of holistic multiculturalism regarding the compatibility of cultural rights with the egalitarian universalism of the constitutional state.[25] The equal protection of the integrity of the individual to which all citizens are entitled includes cultural rights that grant equal access to those social relationships and traditions that are necessary or desirable in order to develop or safeguard one's personal identity. A very different problem is posed by the attempts to repair the historical injustice suffered by indigenous peoples who were subjugated and forcibly integrated into colonial societies. Individualistic legal orders are overstrained when morally justified claims for reparations lead to concessions being made to indigenous tribal societies and forms of life that necessitate purchasing collective empowerment at the cost of according collective rights priority over conflicting individual legal claims.

The role of religion in the constitutional state is very different from that of nation or culture. As political power has become secularized, religion has surrendered the function of legitimizing political authorities and orders to philosophical justifications of constitutional principles. Religious traditions that sustain the political culture may often pose a challenge, and sometimes a threat, to the impartial application and development of the system of rights; at the same time, however, they are sources of energy from which a civic ethos, which is also subject to threats from a different direction, draws its vitality. The imperatives of accelerated capitalist modernization create and lead to the spread of mentalities and attitudes capable of eroding the normative consciousness of civil society over time. We cannot be certain that modernity will always be able to draw upon its own cultural reserves – namely, the canonical ideas of self-consciousness, self-determination and self-realization – for the inspiration and strength it needs to renew itself through solidary movements. Western modernity was again and again sustained by phases of dialectical appropriation of a tradition that it simultaneously kept at a distance.

However, religion occupies a special place among the forces of tradition. On the one hand, these 'strong' traditions dating back to the Axial Age recommend themselves in virtue of their enduring power to shape civilization. By prematurely reducing the complex diversity of public voices, the constitutional state could deprive society of scarce resources for founding meaning and identity. On the other hand, the democratic constitution is a product of a secularization of state power that neutralizes the political influence of churches and religious communities. The institutions of the state equipped with the means of legitimate force for implementing their decisions must not be exposed to the conflicts between competing religious communities. This ambivalent position explains the ongoing controversies over the role of religion in the public sphere, quite apart from the occasions for such controversies currently provided by fundamentalist regression. In connection with the American discussion on the 'public use of reason' by democratic citizens, I drew attention to the complementary learning processes that the democratic state implicitly expects from both its secular and its religious citizens.[26]

IV. Constitutionalization of International Law?

In 1989–90, political observers experienced a strange gestalt switch: political events were no longer structured from the perspective of the competition between two social systems. After the replacement of the bipolar global order by the supremacy of the victorious superpower, the sharply defined reference system of social theory was displaced by older, still unclear models of international law and international politics. This new perspective also informs my detailed interview with Michael Haller from the turn of the year 1990–1.[27] The first Gulf War made me aware of problems that have informed my subsequent work in political theory. The expanded spectrum of themes goes beyond the nation-state framework that still shaped my reflection on democracy and legal theory in *Between Facts and Norms*.

At that time, the explosive situation was already taking shape in which no state, not even the superpower, would be able to master the complexity of world society on its own.[28] And the international legal dimension of the Gulf War, which revived the controversy over humanitarian interventions, inspired hopes that the United Nations would play a more active role. I argued that a reformed world order would make a 'global domestic policy'[29] possible without transforming the central institutions of the United Nations into a world government. European unification also acquired renewed importance against this background; world history seemed to grant a united Europe 'a second chance'.[30] The nation-states were being drawn into the interdependencies of a highly complex world society becoming more closely integrated at an accelerated pace. The system of sovereign states that had taken shape with the Peace of Westphalia in 1648 lost its sharp contours. At the time I still lacked the term 'postnational constellation' that would determine the research agenda in the field of International Relations in the following years.[31]

The interview also touched on a key issue of the international discourse on human rights: 'Are the principles of international law so closely intertwined with the standards of Western rationality ... that such principles are of no use for the nonpartisan adjudication of international conflicts?'[32] On another occasion I addressed this question in the context of the debate over so-called

Asian values being conducted at the time.[33] In that text I defend the universalist claim of human rights against doubts concerning the feasibility of 'justice between nations', whether based on a critique of reason or on a critique of power. Notwithstanding the fact that human rights emerged in the West, the latter can be only one party among others in this discourse. The West must learn from the penetrating scrutiny of its traditions by others to recognize the possible blind spots in its own interpretations of human rights.

In the light of the US invasion of Iraq in violation of international law, I used a rough sketch of the history of international law in an attempt to make the notion of the constitutionalization of international law fruitful for the idea of a global domestic politics without a world government.[34] Kant's philosophy of law again provides the starting point for the conceptual clarification of the transition from the legal order based on states to a cosmopolitan legal order. This perspective also brings to light 'accommodating' trends in the dimensions of international law, political institutions and society – despite the regression of international politics to a condition of social Darwinism since 2001.

Since the founding of the United Nations, the *innovations in international law* have extended above all to the recognition of the prohibition of violence and to the obligation to enforce human rights internationally. Human rights violations have prompted the implicit recognition of individual citizens as subjects of international law, the abolition of the presumption of innocence for sovereign states and the criminal liability of government officials; and, finally, the inclusive membership of the UN commits all states to the Charter and the Declaration of Human Rights. These developments are reflected at the level of legal dogmatics in the change in meaning of basic concepts of international law. In UN documents, the concept of 'sovereignty', for example, means an *empowerment of the state by the international community*. As agents of this community, sovereign states have an obligation to guarantee the basic rights of their citizens, such that they would be held accountable before the International Criminal Court for failing to do so.

The most striking *institutional innovations*, aside from the UN itself, are the elaboration of international jurisprudence, the formation of a supranational entity such as the European Union and the increasingly dense network of international organizations within and outside the United Nations. On the path to *governance beyond the national state*, practices are becoming established that relativize state law and also tacitly contribute to a change in the meaning of the classical concepts of compulsory law and legal validity. Finally, these political and legal innovations can be understood as a response to a *social dynamic* that necessitates the construction of supranational capacities for action. The increasing interdependencies within world society are creating a need for regulations that go beyond mere coordination and call for political procedures for balancing and generalizing interests over extended timescales.

These developments encouraged me to emphasize the necessary theoretical orientations for the design of a global multilevel system.[35] The three elements of statehood, the democratic constitution and civic solidarity that are interconnected in the exemplary form of the constitutional state would have to be unbundled in the course of the constitutionalization of international law and be rearranged at *the different levels of the politically constituted world society*. At the same time, the tasks of a transnationally negotiated global domestic policy of relevance for distribution call for quite different arrangements from those demanded by violations of international security and human rights, which must ultimately be treated as criminal offences at the supranational level of the United Nations.

Thomas Nagel's objection to any political constitution for world society, even one which remains below the organizational threshold of a world state, drew my attention to a further argument. The nation-states, which remain the most important actors on the supranational and international stage so far, are the primary candidates for the role of a driving force of a worldwide constitutionalization process. This provides a reason to adapt constitutional theory to this fact and to extend the concept of the constituent power in such a way that it includes states as well as citizens. Within the framework of the constituted world society, these *states*, in addition to the sum total of world citizens, would also have to be recognized as *subjects of the global constitution*. With this, however, two competing and equally legitimate justice perspectives would find their way into the global constitution. Against the abstract claim to equal treatment of the cosmopolitan citizens, national governments can derive claims for a partially differential treatment from the right of self-preservation of states in which *the equal realization of citizens' liberties had already assumed an exemplary form*. Ultimately, it would be the same citizens who would adopt one of these perspectives in their possibly competing roles as *state* citizens and as *world* citizens. The aforementioned outline argues that this competition should not be dealt with in the abstract as a problem of a theory of justice; rather, it must be mediated by fairly institutionalized political processes themselves.[36]

5

Critique of Reason

Philosophy as it originated with Plato was wisdom and
science in one. It shared with the other Asiatic wisdom
teachings and religions its own path to salvation in the
guise of the contemplative ascent to the Ideas, which it
would later abandon in the collaboration with Christian
theology. From the beginning, it lacked roots in the
rituals of the Greek cities, so that philosophy, unlike
Confucianism and Buddhism, established itself exclusively as an academic activity. This may explain in part
why it was initially understood as foundational science
and why it has maintained a special proximity to the sciences up to the present day. Modern science developed
under the guardianship of philosophical thinking; but
since the seventeenth century science has liberated itself
from this original unity with philosophy.[1] Nowadays
philosophy still sees itself as a scientific activity; but
when the predicate 'scientific' is attached to philosophical argumentation it no longer means that philosophy
can be subsumed under science or that it is a 'normal'
science alongside others.

If what qualifies an academic discipline as normal is
that it has settled on a method and an object domain
defined by basic concepts, then the difference between
philosophy and science is that philosophy is 'non-
settled thinking'. By distancing itself in a further stage

of reflection from every form of knowledge arrived at *intentione recta*, philosophy makes as it were an 'uninhibited' use of a basic feature of human cognition, namely second-order thinking or reflection. This also explains the specific danger of philosophical thought: bad philosophy is betrayed by a self-indulgent use of reflection, by 'empty reflection'. If it is not to get lost in the endless loop of infinite regress, philosophy must find a foothold in questions posed by life instead of losing its way in internally generated problems. Philosophy promises to provide a very abstract form of enlightenment about ourselves. At any rate, the point of reference that redeems the choice of philosophical problems from arbitrariness is the '*self*' of a process of reaching a *self-understanding*.

Whereas science focuses exclusively on an object domain, philosophy keeps its eye at the same time on the insight provided by a corresponding learning processes, that is, on what the knowledge we have acquired about the world (including the human being as another entity in the world) means 'for us'. It operates in a dimension in which changes in our understanding of the world and of ourselves interact. To be sure, because the human sciences gain access to their object domains through interpretation, they also refer to facts constituted in the lifeworld in which this centring reference to 'us' is inscribed. But when the humanities and the social sciences thematize the self-referential function they implicitly fulfil for a contemporary audience, and when they explicitly pursue such an influence disguised as academic studies, they violate the requirement of objectivity. Thus, to take a drastic example, historical research must not be confused with the politics of history and memory. Only philosophy does not need to be ashamed of its self-referential function. Philosophy does not ensure the objectivity of its scientific reflection by obscuring the reflexive reference to an *inclusive 'we'* but on the contrary by *generalizing* it. The 'self' of the self-understanding to be clarified through philosophical reflection is not a particular nation, a particular era, a particular generation, or even an individual – unless it is a question of this person in general. Something acquires 'philosophical' meaning for us insofar as it is 'of existential relevance for us as human beings'. The self-understanding of modernity retains philosophical importance in this sense only through a reference to history as a whole.

However, nothing could have been more alien to the 'sceptical generation' (Schelsky) who began their studies in post-war Germany than the haughty mentality and pretension of exclusivity of the learned representatives of the German-Greek humanist tradition. Nothing seemed more ludicrous to us in the light of the moral corruption of the German university than the claim of 'great' philosophy to cure the world from a single fixed vantage point. We had been inoculated against the pretentiousness and elitism of the claim to a privileged access to the truth. This nimbus of the initiated may also explain why I was repelled by the aura of 'ultimate questions'.[2] When it came to defusing false pretensions, however, a different motive was decisive: only by adopting the egalitarian path of argumentation and enlightenment could we become contemporaries of a modern era that had remained inaccessible to my generation until 1945 in the domains of art and literature, of philosophy and science and of law and politics.

After the war, we encountered 'enlightenment' mainly in the form of the impressive intellectual development from Kant to Marx. We had to take the final step from Hegel to Marx on our own, however, stimulated by studies such as Löwith's book *From Hegel to Nietzsche*. 'Enlightenment' in the present context does not refer to progress in scientific knowledge as such, but rather to an improvement of our self-understanding as a consequence of a specific advance in knowledge about the world. Science is the medium of a form of enlightenment understood by Herder, Humboldt, and Hegel as a liberating process of intellectual formation. Hegel's extravagant attempt to reconstitute the fragmented unity of philosophy and science in terms of an absolute spirit provoked the criticism of the Young Hegelians and led to a 'rupture in nineteenth-century thought' (Löwith). Since then philosophy has been looking for traces of reason in the contingencies of history. Feuerbach and Marx transposed Hegel's 'reality which has become rational' into the status of a historically evolved *potential* of rationality still awaiting its practical realization. In the process, they restored to world history the dimension of an open future while still conceiving of it as a process of intellectual formation. And with the topos of 'the realization of philosophy', they associated an idea that I adopted at the time, namely that philosophy can no longer be understood as such, but only as *criticism*.[3]

After Hegel, the theory of society inherited from the philosophy of history the task of a self-understanding of the present. It tried to identify in the succession of social formations the accumulated potentials of rationality that are blocked for the moment. This theory differs from other social sciences, therefore, not only in virtue of its more comprehensive categorial framework (which until Talcott Parsons also included cultural anthropology, economics and political science), but also in virtue of its 'practical intention' to provide an empirically based, but nevertheless future-oriented, diagnosis of the present. Of course, however empirically well-founded such diagnoses may be, they are not possible without a normative yardstick that is in need of justification.

With his concept of the 'critique of ideology', Marx developed such a yardstick based on the idea of a self-reflexive dissolution of systematic prejudices. Dispelling action-guiding illusions through reflection liberates subjects from social constraints, leading to an increase in autonomy at the level of political action. According to this conception, progress in the dimension of freedom and repression is a result of the subversive work of a self-reflexive activity of which traces can be found in historical formations of consciousness. As late as 1971, I still described the theoretical structure of Marx's conception of social evolution as a twofold process of 'self-reflection of history': 'In reflecting on its context of emergence and anticipating its context of application, theory understands itself as a necessary catalytic moment of the social context it is analysing; specifically, it analyses this context from the perspective of its possible abolition as one pervaded by force and constraint.'[4] In the same text, I also raise objections that this conception fails to address. The reification of the 'self' of self-reflection into the 'species subject' leads to a mistaken transposition of the notion of a 'formation process' as it applies to individual life histories onto history as a whole, with the result that subjects writ large replace intersubjectively shared forms of life.[5]

Once I had replaced these concepts, still rooted in the philosophy of consciousness, with the conceptual tools of 'communicative action' and 'rational discourse', I was able to develop a more differentiated concept of self-reflection than the one which features in *Knowledge and Human Interests*. I realized that the *conventional* way of reconstructing the implicit knowledge of competent speaking, judging and acting subjects that for them is initially only performatively present must not be confused with the kind of critique of forms of self-deception that is intended to *bring the latter to consciousness*. This distinction between 'reconstruction' and 'critique' only reminds us of philosophy's original task of making the propositional content of that kind of tacit knowledge explicit which guides our cognitive and grammatical operations. And because 'this type of knowledge has always claimed the status of a special, of a "pure" knowledge',[6] I could no longer identify philosophy with 'criticism'. During the 1970s, therefore, I developed the *Theory of Communicative Action* based on a different understanding of philosophy. For, once social theory is no longer based on a notion of *emancipatory self-reflection* but instead on a conception of *communicative reason*, 'metaphilosophical' reflection also takes a different direction.[7] Metaphilosophical reflections are now more concerned with differentiating the various tasks and roles that I had bundled together in the over-politicized notion of 'critique'.

I. Metaphilosophical Reflections

A relatively early reflection on the question 'Does philosophy still have a purpose?' dating from 1971 marks the starting point of this development.[8] To Adorno's nostalgic response, which wants to remain faithful to metaphysics even while abandoning it, this essay opposes the more sober assessment that a new constellation is taking shape today in the relationship between philosophy and science, on the one hand, and between philosophy and religion, on the other. However, this conclusion also proves to be ambivalent. The philosophical schools that still existed at the time were living off the prestige of the 1920s which, as we now recognize, was the most productive phase in German philosophy since 1800. On the one hand, the text betrays the satisfaction that Germany during the period of the social-liberal coalition had for the first time become 'a contemporary of Western Europe'; but no less apparent is the regret over the disappearance of the erratic non-conformism of figures like Heidegger and Carl Schmitt, Lukács, Bloch and Benjamin, which had characterized German philosophy in the 1920s. The physiognomy of these unbridled forms of thought that had already been dismissed elsewhere was particularly manifest in a sensitivity towards those losses in human substance that are always the price to be paid for the gains of accelerating modernization processes. The distinguishing features of this period, which at the time of writing lay in the past, had been the critical stance adopted by philosophy towards its time and its ambitious goal of developing a 'theory of the present age', but at the same time the narcissistic gesture of the academic teachers and the idiosyncratic embodiment of philosophical thought in the style and habitus of stubborn individuals.

Compared to this generation of teachers, in the early 1970s I noticed the trends towards the assimilation of philosophy to science which, in spite of the French postmodernists, have now in fact prevailed: on the one hand, the depersonalization of philosophical ideas (and a corresponding waning of philosophical schools) and, on the other, the changeover from seminar discussions as part of research-based university teaching to the problem-solving modus operandi of institutionalized research as the context in which philosophical thought develops. This disciplinary integration of philosophy into the science system as one subject among others only concerns its esoteric role. The reflections on its exoteric role that I presented in the 1970s are very much a product of their time.

I argued that philosophy should adopt a twofold 'critical' stance: against technocratic notions of scientific and technological progress directed by the state, and against certain 'irrational' consequences of a seemingly steady but mentally derailed process of secularization. The claim was that secular enlightened philosophy, in view of the so-called 'new' religious movements and sects set free by the counterculture at the time, should be understood as the true heir to the utopian substance of the Jewish-Christian tradition, and should marshal standards of individualist egalitarianism as a counter-weight to the feared erosion of moral consciousness. In other words, philosophy was supposed to engage in the critique of reason towards both sides: it had to clarify its relationship both to religion and to the sciences and their applications, and it had to contribute to clarifying the self-understanding of modernity. On this basis, it was supposed to play a public role in the context of a liberal political culture – namely, as the 'guardian of rationality' which remains aware of its fallibility.

In stark contrast to this diagnosis, however, in the course of the 1970s, it ceased to be fashionable to understand 'critique of reason' in the twofold sense of a *genitivus objectivus* and a *genitivus subjectivus*; instead, it came to be understood as one-sided criticism 'of' reason as a suspicious object that *necessarily generates* fundamentalist misperceptions of its own achievements. Against this view, I defend the critique of reason in the Kantian sense of *self*-enlightenment concerning the correct – i.e. self-critical – use of reason.[9] The critique of fundamentalism is right only insofar as it insists that philosophical reflection remains a secondary undertaking. Philosophy cannot and should not pretend to play the role of a foundational science for the science system as a whole; instead of *assigning proper places* to other disciplines, in some cases philosophy can try at best to move in step with the development of sciences – which only observe their own methods and the self-propelling force of their own problems – in order to *hold a place open* for strong theoretical strategies. Because I was thinking of the day-to-day research at a Max Planck institute at the time and emphasized the cooperative role of philosophy, this essay does not accord sufficient importance to the *specific contribution* that philosophy must develop on its own and bring to the division of labour – namely, the conceptual work of rational reconstruction as performed by its own core disciplines.

In this regard, philosophy not only engages in exchanges with the sciences. The conceptual analysis performed in the fields of logic, epistemology, the philosophy of language or the theory of action, etc., reveals the proximity to common sense, namely to the everyday know-how of competent judging, speaking and acting subjects. Philosophy stands in an intimate, but at the same time critical, relation to the intuitive background of the performatively present lifeworld, because it makes the practical knowledge that we 'always already know' explicit, thereby removing it from the performative mode of everyday knowledge.[10] That relationship to the lifeworld ensures that even postmetaphysical thinking retains a reference to the whole – if not to the hypostatized totality of beings, then at least to the diffuse and impenetrable pre-theoretical context of our performatively shared historical, social and cultural environment, in whose horizon we find ourselves located as a contingent matter.

The reference to the whole also explains how philosophy can *retain* a function for self-understanding notwithstanding all of the developments towards the scientific objectivation of all domains. It never lets the discourse of modernity completely out of its hand, even if at times it shifts to social theory. In the discourse of modernity, it must respect the autonomous logics of the differentiated 'value spheres' (Max Weber) of science and technology, law and morality, and art and art criticism, just as it must respect the autonomy of any discipline within the science system. But because it reconstructs the rational core of these pre-existing cultural and social structures, it becomes 'multilingual' in a way which qualifies it to play the role of an *interpreter* in the public sphere who mediates between the expert cultures and between the latter and the lifeworld.

As long as philosophy does not regress completely to an academic discipline, it responds, however reservedly, to the need for orientation of modern societies and thus maintains its practical relevance. But the assignment of the sober role of a stand-in or 'placeholder' within, and that of an 'interpreter' outside the science system leaves open the question that the Young Hegelians had answered by inverting the classical relationship between *theory and practice*: can philosophy contribute to a *transforming* political practice? After all, this was how the theme of the relationship between theory and practice had acquired a clear political – specifically, a *social-critical* – meaning. In the context of an existing democratic order, however, this question must assume a reformist tenor, because the constitutional state can be understood as the project of an ever more complete realization of human rights, but at the same time binds its self-transformation to established legal procedures.[11]

Especially in times of crisis, the sceptical question of what enlightenment a critical social theory can still provide becomes insistent. In an interview with Michael Haller following the upheaval of 1989–90, I explain why for the *Theory of Communicative Action* 'emancipation' can no longer play the role of a key concept: it now lacks the backing of a presumptuous philosophy of history.[12] Highly abstract social theories can at best sensitize us to countervailing trends and teach us to understand these ambivalences as appeals to our growing responsibilities to act in view of shrinking opportunities for intervention. To be sure, times of crisis are not only perplexing but also sharpen our vision for the kinds of problems that can be solved through collective action – although they can be solved only if the established parameters of public discussion change to allow new political alternatives to be entertained.

'After the fiasco of a theory that evidently became practical in the wrong way', I addressed the issue of 'Theory and Praxis' once again in an attempt to explain the connection between philosophy and democracy.[13]

Both arose in the same historical context and remain functionally interconnected. Therefore, it is not surprising to find philosophers today not only assuming the special roles of 'experts' or 'life coaches', but also the role of political intellectuals. Philosophers will play this role all the more willingly if they share a dynamic understanding of the democratic constitution as the project of *exhausting* the normative content of the constitutional principles in different, and possibly better, ways under changed historical circumstances. Like any other science, however, philosophy is a fallibilistic enterprise and does not endow intellectuals who use their philosophical insights with any legitimacy that goes beyond their qualification as citizens.

II. Postmetaphysical Thinking

Even after the turn to the theory of communication, I start from a Young Hegelian interpretation of the recent history of philosophy. According to this interpretation, Kant devalued the specific class of arguments on which metaphysics had drawn; with the transition from the 'subjective' to the 'objective' mind, Hegel then took a step towards the critique of the philosophy of consciousness insofar as he recognized the philosophical significance of the new interest in history, culture and society. After the break with idealism, this detranscendentalization of the mind made possible the empirically informed search for the symbolic embodiments of a form of reason historically situated in sociocultural forms of life. Postmetaphysical thinking enlightened by historicism and pragmatism upholds the universalism of the Kantian heritage insofar as it defends a weak and fallibilistic but non-defeatist conception of reason. Reason also remains one and the same even as it is diffused in the medium of languages and symbolic forms.

This position needs to be justified as much against a more or less weakened continuation of totalizing metaphysical thinking as it does against the contextualism of a self-referentially radicalized critique of reason.

The fact that this kind of postmetaphysical thinking upholds the universalist validity claims of reason explains the twofold defensive posture of postmetaphysical thinking. Reason understood in communicative terms affirms a procedural unity in the transitory diversity of its voices. The theme of 'unity and diversity',[14] which has been a central preoccupation of philosophy from the beginning, arises in different forms in the ontological, mentalistic and linguistic paradigms, respectively. The problem cannot be convincingly solved either genetically – through the emergence of the many from the one – or functionally – through the synthetic performances of the mind that establishes unity in diversity – or dialectically – by overcoming conflicting perspectives. It can be solved only in a constructive way, namely through the anticipatory power of the shared counterfactual presuppositions of participants in conversation.

In fact, partners in conversation, however much they may be strangers to each other, can in principle learn from each other in discourse and can at the same time test what they have learned through their dealings with the world that they jointly assume to be objective. This fact that learning *from one another* is interconnected with learning *from the world* would be inexplicable unless concepts such as truth, rationality or justification played *the same pragmatic role* in every linguistic community, albeit in different interpretations, and in this way facilitated a *shared* orientation to the goal of reaching an understanding about context-transcending validity claims.

Dieter Henrich's philosophical life's work, whose aim is to develop a metaphysics after Kant, represents a challenge for the thesis of the transition to post-metaphysical thinking. My controversy with Henrich[15] deserves attention in this context of a general clarification of the status of postmetaphysical thinking.[16] In its classical manifestations, metaphysics belongs to those strong traditions that interpret the world or world history in a homologous way to the holistic structure of the lifeworld centred on us. But modern philosophy, which still maintains a privileged relationship with the lifeworld, can represent this totality only as a *pre-reflexive* background. This explains the break with metaphysical and religious *worldviews* that represent the simultaneously encompassing and receding horizon of the lifeworld as an *objective* totality. In addition, the basic conceptions of metaphysical and religious teachings depend on a fusion of validity claims that has been dissolved in the meantime by the irreversible differentiation between factual knowledge, on the one side, and moral-practical insights and aesthetic judgements, on the other.

A post-Kantian metaphysics that takes the epistemic relation to self in self-consciousness as its starting point tries to avoid the metaphysical objectification of nature and history as a whole, while nevertheless continuing the idealist line of thought geared to an encompassing unity. In the process it encounters two problems that have imposed themselves in the course of the nineteenth century. On the one hand, philosophy finds itself compelled to reconcile Kant with Darwin and Einstein, and in general to bring the individual's self-understanding into harmony with naturalistic self-descriptions. On the other hand, the rise of the social sciences and the humanities, the challenge from history and the intrusion of historical consciousness into philosophy have shaken the foundations of the mentalistic paradigm. The detranscendentalization of consciousness has robbed the epistemic relation to self of its key strategic role for theory-building.

I have examined this movement of thought under the headings of the 'linguistic turn', 'situating reason' and 'procedural rationality'.[17] With this, the relevant reasons for the devaluation of metaphysical models are indicated, even though the merely rough sketch of metaphysical thought does not, of course, do justice to the substance of the Greek, and especially the Aristotelian, heritage that postmetaphysical thinking has taken on board. Besides, the inversion of the classical relationship between theory and practice gives rise to a 'deflation of the extraordinary' in which the one-sidedness of the philosophical tradition had revealed itself – namely, the concentration on the representational function of language and the reduction of reason to its descriptive or theoretical function.

This kind of 'logocentrism' remained harmless at the practical level as long as the 'theory' was written with a capital 'T' and promised to provide the acting subjects with the necessary orientation in their lives. Metaphysics derives an aura from this implicit function, a remnant of which German idealism kept alive in the era of 'Bildungshumanismus'. The loss of this aura is a belated sign that, since the seventeenth century, philosophy has lost its ability to create worldviews. From the perspective of the critique of reason, this raises the question of what philosophy, on a deflated postmetaphysical conception, still has to offer.

In this regard, it is far from clear that there is, as Apel claims, a trend towards the 'Western privileging of the logos'. A line of argumentation going back to Hume suggests an exclusive alliance between philosophy and the sciences, and especially with those that count in each case as the most advanced and as paradigmatic. The corresponding position in practical philosophy is the reduction of reason to a narrow concept of rational choice. On the other hand, the same trend can also solicit a warning against irrationalism to which such a reduced form of theoretical reason gives rise. Therefore, an opposite line of argumentation going back to Kant insists on differentiating between various dimensions of a postmetaphysically deflated and equally secular conception of reason. Kant gathered together the *disjecta membra* of the defeated speculative reason and reassembled them on the basis of his critique of metaphysics. Today, this philosophy encounters two opposed approaches: on the one side, a scientistic version of naturalism that modernizes the nineteenth- and early twentieth-century 'scientific image of the world' with borrowings from biogenetics and neurobiology, robotics and neo-Darwinian evolutionary theory; and, on the other side, an ambiguous revival of religion that discharges in fundamentalist violence and at the same time serves as a source of unsurpassed semantic potentials. These oppositions revive the critical question of the self-understanding of postmetaphysical thinking.

III. The Challenge of Naturalism

The scientistic view that physical knowledge or knowledge of this kind is all that ultimately 'counts' is a source of embarrassment for philosophy. Even for philosophers who share this view, all that remains is to adopt the style of 'hard' science. However, such mimicry does not turn conceptual analysis into an empirical science. My initial response to the challenge of naturalism was to develop a genealogy of postmetaphysical thinking.[18]

If we assume that today the work of philosophy consists essentially in explaining general competences and in reflection on the distinctive logics of the differentiated cultural formations, the lifeworld suddenly becomes a general theme that, in the far-advanced internal differentiation of the discipline, still holds together the diverging hyphen-philosophies. On the one hand, the performative knowledge of competent judging, speaking and acting subjects is rooted in the *underlying* structure of a lifeworld. The latter can be understood as the ensemble of enabling conditions for the competences that distinguish human beings as sociocultural creatures – namely, the ability to adopt an intentional relation to the world and to engage in reciprocal perspective-taking, to use propositionally differentiated languages for the purposes of communication and representation and to engage in instrumental action and social cooperation. On the other hand, this general structure of the lifeworld is objectified in the diversity of historically *existing* forms of life, including social practices and cultural forms of science and technology, law and morality, and art and criticism.

From the perspective of a concept of the lifeworld based on the theory of communication, Husserl's attempt to uncover the 'forgotten meaning foundation' of the sciences by recourse to this lifeworld provides a point of contact for the controversy with naturalism. At the same time, however, the genealogical question of the origin of this concept in the processing of the metaphysical and religious heritage of the Axial Age undercuts the transcendental distinction which informs Husserl's diagnosis that the scientistic understanding of the sciences is based on an objectivist self-misunderstanding. From the perspective of the path 'from worldviews to the lifeworld', it is by no means evident that the epistemic role of the lifeworld must be understood in transcendental terms as the background for the creation of scientific object domains. For only in that case would it erect an *insuperable* barrier to a scientific revision of the self-understanding of persons operative in everyday life. Yet in fact, the genealogy of postmetaphysical thinking makes it clear that a lifeworld *displaced* into transcendental consciousness and *elevated* into the intelligible sphere can emerge *as such* only by way of a detranscendentalization of reason.

The conceptual constellation of 'lifeworld', 'objective world' and 'everyday world' serves for me as the key to a rough analysis of the development of worldviews. From the conventional viewpoint of the 'scientific image of the world', this development appears as a progressive cognitive unbundling of the objective world knowable by science from those projections in which aspects of the lifeworld actually operating only behind us in the background appear as structuring parts of the objective world in front of us. Philosophy played an important role in dissolving these projections by first working out an ontological concept of the world as the totality of entities and then, since the seventeenth century, by developing a concept of the world as the totality of representable objects. This trend towards objectivization, which began with the *modern natural sciences*, seems to boil down to the assumption that a radical, scientistic form of naturalism has the last word.

However, this conception fails to do justice to a different trend, which begins with the *humanities and social sciences*, towards objectivizing the sectors of the everyday world constituted by the lifeworld. Since then, our image of the objective world has become polarized because the objectivization of everyday phenomena points *in different directions*. 'Objectivization' must not be confused automatically with tailoring natural processes in the world to the dimension of dealings with manipulable and measurable phenomena. Whereas natural science approaches the idea of impartial judgement by *eliminating* the lifeworld qualities of the everyday world, the human sciences can aspire to the same goal only via the *hermeneutic confirmation and deepening reconstruction* of lifeworld experiences and practices. This bipolar objectivization complicates the project of a naturalization of the mind because the intersubjective constitution of a symbolically structured mind could prevent the cognitive sciences from tracing subjective experiences *directly* back to operations of the brain. If one wants to do justice to the shaping of 'subjective' by the 'objective mind', one must accord priority in the sequence of causal explanation to *intersubjectively shared* acts and contexts of meaning which, as Putnam puts it, are 'nothing in the head' of single actors.

This is the thrust of the line of argument developed in an essay on 'Free Will',[19] which takes the ongoing controversy as an occasion to argue for a weaker version of naturalism as an alternative to scientism. There is an epistemic gap between a mode of access from the observer perspective to the world of physically measurable states and events and a hermeneutic mode of access to symbolic objects and practices of the lifeworld tied to the participant perspective. The dualism of the corresponding language games must be taken seriously because the one is not reducible to the other. The failed attempts to translate propositions from intentionalist into physicalist language reveal differences between competing descriptions of supposedly identical objects that cannot be bridged at the semantic level. Nor can the failures of reductionism be defused by a compatibilist approach: the human brain does not 'think'! On the other hand, we feel the need for a coherent image of the universe that includes human beings as natural entities. This is what motivates the search for the conceptual dimension of a *natural history* in which the initial conditions for sociocultural learning processes reconstructed 'from above' through conceptual analysis can be identified with a specific constellation of natural traits and behaviours. Such a 'correspondence' would have to be established, for example, via the semantic bridge of a sufficiently abstract concept of 'learning' and 'development' that establishes a conceptual continuum between the categories of sociocultural learning and learning in terms of natural evolution.[20]

IV. The Challenge of Religion

The detachment of postmetaphysical thinking from metaphysics went hand-in-hand with an emancipation from subordination to theology. The discourses of epistemology and of social contract theory that have been authoritative since then crystallize around the two innovations of the era, namely the experimental and mathematic sciences and the bureaucratic power of the secular state. Out of these discourses developed, finally, the at once scientific and secular self-understanding of the Enlightenment. Philosophy allies itself with the sciences, which it must allow to follow their own course; at the same time, by adopting a critical stance towards religion and metaphysics, it also turns its back on its own past. However, the methodological assumption *etsi Deus non daretur* does not have any specific implications for the nature and content of the critique of religion.

While Hobbes and the *encyclopédistes* looked for explanations for religious errors and illusions – in other words, for a truth *about* religion – Spinoza and the German idealists searched for truths *in* religion (notwithstanding differences in their respective characterizations of the world of religious ideas as a whole). To be sure, Kant and Hegel claimed for philosophy the right to distinguish what is true from what is false in the contents of the Christian tradition. But in order to discover this, they had to take the competing claims to truth in both fields seriously; they had to regard religion as an intellectual formation on a par with art and literature. They, too, formed a secular concept of religion, but they were not interested in the functions or causes of religious ideas in general. Rather, they assumed that the philosophy of religion should fill a gap in a conception of the human mind whose analysis would otherwise remain incomplete. Kant's concept of pure rational religion is intended to answer questions left open by his moral philosophy. And, with his conception of religion as a form of absolute spirit, Hegel makes philosophy aware of the origins of its own religious contents that it has raised to the conceptual level.

My reflection on the dialogical relationship between these philosophers and the Christian heritage rests on the observation that Kant's critique of reason, for example, does not remain impartial between religion and metaphysics.[21] Whereas his transcendental dialectic consists in restricting theoretical reason to the use of the understanding guided by experience and to reining in the excesses of speculative reason through a devastating critique of metaphysical traditions, his philosophy of religion is by no means restricted to the destructive business of a corresponding critique of religious traditions. On the contrary, it also pursues the task of *making practical reason aware of religious sources* from which it can learn something about the precarious connection between the worthiness of a morally meritorious person to be happy and her *justified* hope that she will in fact experience a corresponding level of happiness. The task of the philosophy of religion is to decipher the concept of the 'highest good' belonging to moral philosophy as a translation of the biblical eschatological notion of the 'kingdom of God on earth'; Kant thereby draws attention to a deficit that cannot be overcome within the framework of his moral theory.

As rational beings, we are interested in promoting a final end. However, we can imagine the 'agreement of morality with happiness' only as the result of an intervention by a higher power, because the human understanding can never foresee the cumulative interconnections between the contingent side effects of *individually enjoined* moral actions. Kant thought that he could postulate such a power because we are morally obliged to promote the highest good (and nobody can be morally required to do anything impossible). In fact, however, the problem is that Kant turns the promotion of the highest good, which would be possible only through cooperative action, into a duty in the first place. The excessiveness of this requirement transcends the boundaries of a rational morality, which is addressed to the free will of each individual person. Each individual has an 'immediate' relation to the moral law. However, this objection clearly reveals a deficit that Kant wants to make good in the philosophy of religion.

A morality that obligates the individual person shuts itself off from the public dimension of a shared enterprise; there are good reasons why it cannot make expectations, whose fulfilment requires the active solidarity of a collectivity, into the content of individually addressed moral duties. However, Kant's philosophy of religion deals with the collective contribution that the Church, and the 'People of God' to which it lends institutional form, *ought* to make to 'the foundation of a kingdom of God on earth'. In such passages, practical reason seems to encounter motifs in the biblical tradition whose semantic contents *have not yet been translated into secular concepts* but in which it nevertheless takes an interest.

While Kant draws our attention to contents that secular reason can and should assimilate from religious traditions, Hegel discovered the rich semantic legacy of religious ideas to which philosophy has lent conceptual form. However, both Kant and Hegel were equally convinced that religions have essentially been superseded and that it is exclusively a matter for philosophy to sift out the rational core from this traditional material. The classical works in sociology shared this perspective on religion as a *superseded* intellectual formation and developed a theory of the secularization of society intended to provide an empirical explanation of the disappearance of religious consciousness. The development of European societies seemed to confirm this theory. But the validity of the theory of secularization is now being called into question from an expanded global perspective. The controversy of recent decades has forced us to adopt more nuanced positions and has undermined the self-confident prediction that religion will disappear as society and culture modernize.

Today, the issue of secularization is also connected with the need for political regulation of an emerging multicultural world society.[22] The intercultural discourse now under way on human rights and on generally accepted conceptions of justice must overcome not only the conflict between the religious worldviews but also the antagonisms between religious parties, on the one side, and secularists, on the other. This immediately prompts the philosophical question of how a postmetaphysical form of thought that regards itself as the custodian of reason emancipated from religious guardianship is related to contemporary forms of religion. After all, it is not only pragmatic considerations and empirical reasons that require us to take *political* notice of the continued presence of churches and religious communities. Rather, historical experiences and reflexive insights suggest that today *philosophy* can no longer approach the vital world religions in the role of an inspector who examines the truth content of religious traditions. Not even from a provincial Western perspective can philosophy know whether the learning process through which it assimilated important semantic contents from the Jewish-Christian tradition until now can be *continued* or will even remain *incomplete*. An agnostic philosophy that is nevertheless still willing to learn can enter into a fruitful dialogical relationship with a religion that has become reflexive. While philosophy insists on the boundary between the universes of faith and knowledge and religion refrains from attempts to monopolize philosophy, both parties must acknowledge that dialogue is not a zero-sum game and that it is incompatible with the instrumentalization of the other side. A gain for one side does not necessarily mean a loss for the other.

Under the title 'An Awareness of What is Missing',[23] I advocated such a dialogue and presented reasons for re-examining the situation of postmetaphysical thinking *between* science and religion from the perspective of the critique of reason. The secularistic reason that is *exclusively* critical of religion and *unreservedly* supports scientific progress is transformed in the process into a mode of reflection that defends its autonomy against both sides – against the pull of scientistic assimilation to natural scientific theory-building and against religious dogmatism. However, postmetaphysical thinking can acknowledge as contemporary intellectual formations only those religious traditions and communities which know that their messages must gain a hearing within the differentiated housing of modernity, and only those theologies which also recognize the genealogy of postmetaphysical thinking as a learning process.

From this perspective, dialogues that seek to cross the dividing line between philosophical and theological language games take the place of philosophical explanations of religious thought. The philosophical willingness to learn from contemporary religion must at least assume a dialogical style. To be sure, philosophy of religion understood as the rational self-interpretation of a practised faith using philosophical means has its own merits. But postmetaphysical thinking, for which religious experience and the religious mode of faith retain an opaque core, must dispense with philosophy of religion. Moreover, it does not try to *reduce* the potentially rational content of religious traditions to what it can assimilate according to its own standards through translation into discursive speech. A prime example of this practice is the controversy between Karl Jaspers and Rudolf Bultmann. For more than four decades, I myself have consistently received fruitful impulses from discussions with theologians.

On re-reading my contribution to a conference at the University of Chicago Divinity School in 1988,[24] I was surprised to discover a continuity in my thought that contradicts allegations that I have changed my mind in the meantime.[25] Among other things, I find a reference there to the 'specific barrier' that any false ingratiation of secular reason to religion runs up against. The attempt, supposedly on grounds of displaying authenticity, to borrow promising connotations from the religious vocabulary is not a question of literary style but constitutes a dilution of discursive thought. Ritual practices provide evidence of an early stage in the history of the development of the human mind. Mythical explanations, which attach a meaning to rites, probably already represent a subsequent attempt to interpret a meaning potential embodied in prelinguistic symbols.[26] This mode of consciousness has become inaccessible to us sons and daughters of modernity. The religions alone maintain a connection to those archaic beginnings, even if today the meaning of the communal religious cult is interpreted in highly differentiated theological doctrines. Religion will hardly survive unless it remains rooted in a ritual practice. This is what distinguishes religion from all secular formations of thought even more categorically than any recourse to the authority of revelation. This should serve as a warning against effusive philosophical attempts to transcend the strict boundary between faith and knowledge.

Notes

Introduction

1. Jürgen Habermas, *Philosophische Texte: Studien-ausgabe in fünf Bänden* (Frankfurt am Main: Suhrkamp, 2009) (hereinafter *"Studienausgabe"*). Note that the titles of essays from the *Studienausgabe* are given in bold in footnotes below.)
2. Only four out of a total of forty-six articles are from the 1970s, and none of them is from the 1950s or 1960s.
3. As Habermas states in the two pages that serve as a preface to each of the five volumes of the German edition. He was very well aware of the hard choices he had to make and, thus, of the typically philosophical and thematic character he lent this five-volume edition. This is why the footnotes cite not only his thematically unified works but also all the collections of articles in which he develops his social theory or discusses single authors.
4. Jürgen Habermas, *Autonomy and Solidarity: Interviews with Jürgen Habermas*, rev. edn, ed. Peter Dews (London: Verso, 1992), p. 79: 'I myself am a product of "re-education".' Coming from Habermas's mouth, this formulation also has a provocative political ring for the specific

reason that it was also used in Germany to criti-
cize the occupying forces, their moral pretension
and the brutality of their methods. In Habermas's
mind, by laying claim to the term 're-education',
he was opposing the idea that the Second World
War was a normal war that had been waged,
and subsequently lost, by a normal state now
subjected to a morally illegitimate international
occupation force. Thus, this was also an extension of the amazement and retrospective suspicion
that Habermas felt concerning the years of his
childhood and adolescence between 1929 and
1945, whose conformism and quasi-normality
now struck him as illusory. On a more general
level, embracing re-education also reflected the
desire for a historical break with the cultural background that had fostered Nazism and with the
temptation, inspired by German Romanticism, of
a conception of Germany as belonging to Central
rather than to Western Europe.

5. Habermas studied in turn at the universities in
   Göttingen, Zurich and Bonn. He would later
   describe the intellectual climate of his student
   years as provincial and ambivalent.

6. Karl Löwith, *From Hegel to Nietzsche*, trans.
   David E. Green (New York: Columbia University
   Press, 1964). Habermas cites this book by Löwith
   regularly in his writings into the 2000s – as he does
   here, too, at the beginning of the fifth introduction.

7. This can be seen from his doctoral disserta-
   tion which he defended in Bonn in 1954 under
   Rothacker's direction and which dealt with the
   constellation of the generation following Hegel
   and the inspirational role of Schelling. See
   Habermas, *Das Absolute und die Geschichte:
   Von der Zwiespältigkeit in Schellings Denken*,
   Dissertationsdruck (Neuwied and Berlin, 1954).

8. Karl-Otto Apel, *Transformation der Philosophie*, 2 vols (Frankfurt am Main: Suhrkamp, 1973); English translation of selected essays: *Towards a Transformation of Philosophy*, trans. Glyn Adey and David Frisby (London: Routledge & Kegan Paul, 1980).

9. *Ibid.*, Volume I, pp. 225–77.

10. *Ibid.*, Volume II, pp. 157–77. Prior to this strictly intellectual influence, Habermas's central preoccupation with intersubjectivity had been shaped by two powerful biographical motives: on the one hand, by the retrospective light cast, following the discovery of the camps in 1945, on the illusory semi-normality of the human relationships of his life up to that time and, on the other, by the hardships he had endured as a young child as a result of his cleft lip and palate, which exposed him to painful surgeries and the taunts of his comrades. Viewed in this light, his central preoccupation with communication exhibits a profound emotional and intellectual coherence.

11. Habermas's first major realization is documented by his 1953 article on Heidegger: 'Martin Heidegger: On the Publication of the Lectures of 1935', in Richard Wolin, *The Heidegger Controversy: A Critical Reader* (Cambridge, MA: MIT Press, 1993), pp. 186–97.

12. At least four things should be borne in mind concerning this retrospective suspicion and the theme of the *Sonderweg* [i.e., the view, popular among certain conservative thinkers, that German history and culture represent a 'special path' at variance with the mainstream of Western modernity and the Enlightenment – *Trans.*]: 1. The Nazis appropriated the expressivist and Romantic tropes of harmony and of life as an organic totality, which Herder in particular had opposed to the

mechanism and universalism of the French and
Kantian Enlightenment, and reinterpreted them
in terms of the biologistic and racialist worldview
of National Socialism. These tropes had already
been invested with new meaning by conservative thinkers throughout the nineteenth century
and provided continuous support to an ambivalent attitude towards modernity. 2. The Greek
theme, which had been central since the work of
the art historian Johann Joachim Winckelmann
and its reception by the German Romantics, was
also appropriated in the same way by the Nazis,
who planned, in the style of Spengler's specula-
tions on history and culture, a modernist revival
of Sparta as a counterweight to the historical
dominance of Jerusalem. 3. Alfred Rosenberg's
appeal to Meister Eckhart, Heidegger's defence of
a Platonic meta-political conception in the early
1930s and Schmitt's authoritarian Augustinian
pessimism show that Plato (rather than Nietzsche,
contrary to what is often assumed) was the
official philosopher of the Third Reich. 4. The
neo-Romantic theme of a poetical elite was also
misappropriated by the Nazis in a belligerent,
racial and sacrificial form. Taken together, these
elements explain Habermas's hypersensitivity to
all of the Platonizing and Plotinizing currents
in German intellectual history, which led from
German mysticism to Luther, took an authoritarian turn with the suppression of the peasants'
revolt, combined with Romanticism and German
idealism, and extended up to Heidegger, and even
to Adorno. It is this physiognomy that Habermas
is referring to when he speaks of the 'German
Platonic tradition', with its pessimistic, elitist and
authoritarian traits, which inform a profound
ambivalence towards modernity. This is why he

tends to say that Kant is the only German thinker who does not have an ambiguous relation to modernity.

13. Apel is more sceptical about 'normalization' and less suspicious concerning the German philosophical tradition. This difference is shown, for example, by the commonalities that Habermas sees between Wittgenstein's and Heidegger's respective relations to the German mind; see Habermas, *Texte und Kontexte* (Frankfurt am Main: Suhrkamp, 1991), pp. 84–90.

14. The imperatives and the subsequent success of the post-war economic reconstruction tended to combine trends towards cultural conservatism with the defence of technocratic and capitalist rationalization. This is a very profound trend which, for Habermas, persists to the present day, as can be seen from his criticisms of Deutschmark nationalism and subsequently of Germany's European policy.

15. See Habermas, 'The Analytical Theory of Science and Dialectics' and 'A Positivistically Bisected Rationalism' in Theodor W. Adorno et al., *The Positivist Dispute in German Sociology*, trans. Glyn Adey and David Frisby (London: Heinemann, 1976), pp. 131–62 and 198–225.

16. In his major articles from the 1930s on Critical Theory and its genealogy, Horkheimer defined his position essentially in contrast to Heidegger and to the Vienna Circle, and later from the 1940s to the 1960s in contrast to substantialist positions (such as neo-Thomism) and positivism.

17. Habermas's terminology is somewhat loose when it comes to this sequencing ('paradigm' – 'turn' – 'model') but these three elements can be clearly distinguished in his work. It was inspired beginning in the 1950s, as we have seen, by Löwith and

Apel. It was reinforced in the 1980s by Dummett and Tugendhat who, during the 1970s, discussed at length the new form of philosophy inaugurated by the analysis of language and the resulting historical rupture; by Foucault's analysis in *The Order of Things* of the antinomies of an excessively transcendental position in the wake of the modern caesura; by Rorty's critique of the philosophy of reference in *Philosophy and the Mirror of Nature*; but also, albeit in a very loose sense, by Derrida's revival of the term 'logocentrism' for the critique of the primacy of assertoric over other kinds of propositions.

18. In the early 1980s, Habermas would describe this, in a moment of retrospective reflection on his theory, as the metatheoretical dimension of the puzzle of theoretical construction; see Habermas, *The Theory of Communicative Action*, trans. Thomas McCarthy, 2 vols (Boston, MA: Beacon Press, 1984, 1987), vol. 2, pp. 399–400; and *Moral Consciousness and Communicative Action*, trans. Christian Lenhardt and Shierry Weber Nicholsen (Cambridge: Polity, 1990), pp. 15–16.

19. See below I.B.1 and I.C.1.

20. After graduating from university in Bonn in 1954, Habermas conducted research at the German Research Foundation (DFG) and worked occasionally as a journalist before being recruited by the Institute for Social Research in 1956. In 1955 he married Ute Wesselhoeft, with whom he would have three children.

21. Jürgen Habermas, Ludwig von Friedeburg, Christoph Oehler and Friedrich Weltz, *Student und Politik: Eine soziologische Untersuchung zum politischen Bewusstsein Frankfurter Studenten* (Neuwied and Berlin: Luchterhand, 1961).

22. This generational difference was reflected in their

respective evaluations of the significance of the end of the war. For Habermas, 1945 represented a fundamental break – the historic defeat of fascism – whereas for his elders, Horkheimer, Adorno and Marcuse, the continuity with pre-war conditions dominated: the same bureaucratic society, economically concentrated and cemented by the culture of mass consumption. But this difference was also marked for Habermas by the pessimism and aestheticism of certain Romantic tropes of the German Platonic tradition and thus by an ambivalent relation to modernity that had to be overcome. And, finally, it was reflected in differences between their respective intellectual resources: predominantly German for the older generation (Hegel, Schopenhauer, Marx and Weber), far more eclectic in Habermas's case (pragmatism, American sociology, ordinary language philosophy, etc., in addition to the German references).

23. From this point of view, the decidedly more ambitious theoretical approach of Marcuse in *Eros and Civilization*, especially as regards his interpretation and use of Marx and Freud, seemed to Habermas to be the better example to follow.

24. Habermas, *The Structural Transformation of the Public Sphere: An Inquiry into a Category of Bourgeois Society*, trans. Thomas Burger and Frederick Lawrence (Cambridge: Polity, 1992).

25. Habermas, who was deemed to be too radical by Horkheimer, left the Institute for Social Research in 1959. The book on the transformations of the public sphere, which served as Habermas's habilitation, was supervised by Wolfgang Abendroth, one of the very few left-leaning professors of public law at the time. For Habermas, Abendroth embodied both a form of academic courage and an extension of the spirit of Austro-Marxism that

associated strong democracy with parliamentary institutions.

26. Habermas was inspired, on the one hand, by Reinhart Koselleck and, on the other, by Abendroth, who were exponents, respectively, of criticism as the essence of Enlightenment culture and of a participatory understanding of the constitution. Habermas's understanding of democracy must also be seen in relation to Dewey's participatory and experimental conception of politics.

27. This also highlights indirectly the backwardness of eighteenth-century Germany, which was poorer and more fragmented than Great Britain or France, but also the failure of the 1848 revolution, the subsequent authoritarian modernization under Bismarck and, finally, the technocratic and Keynesian growth of the 1950s.

28. Habermas, *Theory and Practice*, trans. John Viertel (Cambridge: Polity, 1988). See, in particular, pp. 41–81.

29. From Popper Habermas adopted the fallibilistic epistemology bound up with the defence of the open society and with a credible standard of scientificity; and from Gadamer (complementing what he had learned from Apel) the irreducibility (following Aristotle) of practice to instrumental action and hence the irreducibility of its theoretical processing by the understanding in Dilthey's sense. It was Gadamer who welcomed Habermas to Heidelberg as a professor following his habilitation in 1961, where he taught until 1964. In 1964, he returned to Frankfurt as professor of philosophy and sociology, where he would remain until 1971.

30. This path of a genealogy of understanding, leading from Vico to Gadamer via Wilhelm von Humboldt, Wilhelm Dilthey and Heidegger, was

marked out in part by Apel in *Transformation der Philosophie* I, pp. 106–37.

31. See Habermas, *On the Logic of the Social Sciences*, trans. Shierry Weber Nicholsen and Jerry A. Stark (Cambridge: Polity, 1988), p. 106, and note 33 below

32. Habermas, *Technik und Wissenschaft als Ideologie* (Frankfurt am Main: Suhrkamp, 1968); English translation of chs 2–4 in Habermas, *Toward a Rational Society: Student Protest, Science, and Politics*, trans. Jeremy J. Shapiro (Cambridge: Polity, 1986), chs 4–6.

33. Habermas, *Knowledge and Human Interests*, trans. Jeremy J. Shapiro (Cambridge: Polity, 1987), p. 242.

34. Habermas, **'Reflections on the Linguistic Foundations of Sociology: The Christian Gauss Lectures (Princeton University, February–March, 1971)'**, in Habermas, *On the Pragmatics of Social Interaction*, trans. Barbara Fultner (Cambridge: Polity, 2001), pp. 1–103.

35. This is not announced in the Gauss Lectures but only later in the 1970s in Habermas, *The Theory of Communicative Action*, vol. 1, pp. 316–19.

36. See Habermas, *The Theory of Communicative Action*, vol. 2, pp. 64–6.

37. See the retrospective account in Habermas, 'Nach dreißig Jahren: Bemerkungen zu *Erkenntnis und Interesse*', in Stefan Müller-Doohm (ed.), *Das Interesse der Vernunft* (Frankfurt am Main: Suhrkamp, 2000), pp. 12–20.

38. Habermas, *Legitimation Crisis*, trans. Thomas McCarthy (Cambridge: Polity, 1988).

39. Habermas, *Zur Rekonstruktion des Historischen Materialimus* (Frankfurt am Main: Suhrkamp, 1976).

40. The guiding thread is that of convergences between Mead and Kohlberg.

41. This is the theme of his book *Theorie der Gesellschaft oder Sozialtechnologie* (co-authored with Niklas Luhmann) (Frankfurt am Main: Suhrkamp, 1971) and of *Legitimation Crisis*.

42. Habermas, *Legitimation Crisis*.

43. Habermas, *The Philosophical Discourse of Modernity*, trans. Frederick Lawrence (Cambridge: Polity, 1987); *Postmetaphysical Thinking: Philosophical Essays*, trans. William Mark Hohengarten (Cambridge: Polity, 1992); 'Communicative Action and the Detranscendentalized "Use of Reason"', in Habermas, *Between Naturalism and Religion: Philosophical Essays*, trans. Ciaran Cronin (Cambridge: Polity, 2008), pp. 24–76.

44. Habermas, *Postmetaphysical Thinking II: Essays and Replies*, trans. Ciaran Cronin (Cambridge: Polity, 2017).

45. Habermas, *Moral Consciousness and Communicative Action*; *Justification and Application: Remarks on Discourse Ethics*, trans. Ciaran Cronin (Cambridge: Polity, 1990); *Between Facts and Norms*, trans. William Rehg (Cambridge: Polity, 1996).

46. Habermas, *Truth and Justification*, trans. Barbara Fultner (Cambridge: Polity, 2003).

47. Habermas, *Kleine politische Schriften V–XIII* (Frankfurt am Main: Suhrkamp, 1985–2013).

48. Habermas, *The Postnational Constellation*, ed. and trans. Max Pensky (Cambridge: Polity, 2001).

49. Habermas, *The Future of Human Nature*, trans. Hannah Beister, Max Pensky and William Rehg (Cambridge: Polity, 2003).

50. Habermas, *Between Naturalism and Religion*, trans. Ciaran Cronin (Cambridge: Polity, 2008).

51. Habermas, **'Faith and Knowledge'**, in *The Future of Human Nature*, pp. 101–15; but also

Postmetaphysical Thinking II, trans. Ciaran Cronin (Cambridge: Polity, 2017).

52. The reference to Kant has both a German (see the long footnote in I.A.1) and an American dimension, because Rawls described his position as a form of Kantian constructivism and the communitarians brought in particular Aristotelian and Hegelian objections against him. Moreover, Hilary Putnam opposed his Kantian pragmatism to Rorty's sceptical pragmatism.

53. See the various remarks below on the realist readjustment, on ethics and on law.

54. Thus, the fact that Habermas's work began with social theory and that postmetaphysical philosophy does not play the role of a privileged foundational discourse should also make us wary of the image of roots and trunk, which is perhaps somewhat too Cartesian and is offered here in a pedagogical spirit. Sociology enlightens philosophy about its own cultural trajectory within the dynamics of differentiation, just as the choice of sociological concepts is in need of additional philosophical justification. This image of a tree is primarily intended to capture the dynamic dimension of Habermas's work.

55. Because, in contrast to the five volumes of the *Studienausgabe*, the texts to which Habermas refers are not reprinted in the present volume, we will follow Habermas's order of exposition while sometimes discussing the specific content of the articles mentioned by Habermas in greater detail than he does in his introductions.

56. This justification must be the supplemented by one linked to the perspective of detranscendentalization, as discussed above and as we shall see again in II.E. But, as in the case of the theory of law further on, the justification inherent in the process

of theoretical construction itself is also missing. This would be supplied only by the *Theory of Communicative Action*, with the rereading in two series of the classics of sociology and the knitting together in stages of what had to be added to them.

57. Thus, point 1 below corresponds to the beginning and section (1), point 2 to sections (2)–(4), point 3 to sections (5) and (6) and point 4 to section (7) of Habermas's introduction. These groupings are evident in the introduction itself, but can also be read in the table of contents of the five volumes of the *Studienausgabe*.

58. Habermas, 'Reflections on the Linguistic Foundations of Sociology'.

59. Habermas, 'Reflections on the Linguistic Foundations of Sociology', pp. 10–11 and *passim*. Here, typically for Habermas, we have a very impressive *problematized inventory*, which shows that only the proposed solution integrates all of the necessary theoretical advantages. See the remarks on the modalities of theoretical construction in section I.A.3 above.

60. Habermas, 'Actions, Speech Acts, Linguistically Mediated Interactions, and the Lifeworld', in Habermas, *On the Pragmatics of Communication*, ed. and trans. Maeve Cooke (Cambridge: Polity, 2000), pp. 215–55.

61. Habermas, 'Individuation through Socialization', in Habermas, *Postmetaphysical Thinking*, trans. William Mark Hohengarten (Cambridge: Polity, 1992), pp. 149–204.

62. Habermas, 'Aspects of the Rationality of Action', in Theodor F. Geraets (ed.), *Rationality Today* (Ottawa: University of Ottawa Press, 1979), pp. 185–204; Habermas, 'Reconstruction and Interpretation in the Social Sciences', in *Moral*

Consciousness and Communicative Action, pp. 21–42.

63. Three points already mentioned must be borne in mind in this regard. First of all, the reconstruction presupposes a great deal of theoretical puzzle work connected in the vertical dimension with everyday intuitions that must be taken into account. Secondly, this reconstruction presupposes a certain *order* of theoretical production that places the hypotheses that inform criticism *in second position*, as in Chomsky, for whom *additional* hypotheses are required to account for cases that deviate from standard performances. And finally, this reconstructive epistemology and this order also express the intention to rebalance the excessively one-sided and pessimistic theory of rationality and modernity of the first-generation Frankfurt School through a strong, really existing normative core. These three elements must be taken together in order to capture the continuity and breaks with the Weberian Marxism of the first generation.

64. Habermas, 'Conceptions of Modernity: A Look Back at Two Traditions', in *The Postnational Constellation*, pp. 130–56.

65. See Habermas, *The Philosophical Discourse of Modernity*. With regard to this debate, which is replete with very different national resonances, it is important for Habermas that we bear in mind the forms of relativism and contextualism which, since Herder, have been opposed to Kantian rationalism and universalism. Thus, the final section of the first introduction draws a connection with the question of reason.

66. As above, point 1 below corresponds to the beginning and to sections (1) and (2), point 2 to sections (3) and (4), point 3 to sections (5) and (6) and point 4 to section (7) of Habermas's introduction.

67. Habermas, 'Hermeneutic and Analytic Philosophy: Two Complementary Versions of the Linguistic Turn', in *Truth and Justification*, pp. 51–82.

68. Habermas, 'Toward a Critique of the Theory of Meaning', in Habermas, *Postmetaphysical Thinking*, trans. William Mark Hohengarten (Cambridge: Polity, 1992), pp. 57–87. The article referred to here predates the realist turn and represents the earliest form of Habermas's response to contextualism and postmodernism, which he initially considered to be sufficient.

69. Karl Bühler's theory, which distinguishes the three functions of expression, representation and addressing, serves as background corroboration for this unity and Habermas's critique of the one-sidedness of the three types of semantics. And, as we saw above, Habermas generalizes Dummett's theory of justified assertability to the different claims to validity in order to capture their normativity.

70. Habermas, 'Some Further Clarifications of the Concept of Communicative Rationality' (1996), in Habermas, *On the Pragmatics of Communication*, ed. and trans. Maeve Cooke (Cambridge: Polity, 1988), pp. 307–42.

71. This is his response to a serious objection raised by Herbert Schnädelbach in *Zur Rehabilitierung des animal rationale* (Frankfurt am Main: Suhrkamp, 1992).

72. Thus, Apel's critique reinforces that of Schnädelbach; see Karl-Otto Apel, *Auseinandersetzungen in Erprobung des transzendentalpragmatischen Ansatzes* (Frankfurt am Main: Suhrkamp, 1998), p. 732.

73. It should be noted that this readjustment opens up major (unexplored) critical possibilities for Habermas. The realist turn can also have

implications for social criticism (e.g., for analysing negotiations and compromises in the theory of law), and not just for the theory of knowledge or language.

74. Habermas, 'Communicative Reason and the Detranscendentalized "Use of Reason"', in *Between Naturalism and Religion*, pp. 24–76.

75. Habermas, 'Wahrheitstheorien', in Habermas, *Vorstudien und Ergänzungen zur Theorie des kommunikativen Handelns* (Frankfurt am Main: Suhrkamp, 1984), pp. 127–86.

76. Habermas, 'Richard Rorty's Pragmatic Turn', in Robert Brandom (ed.), *Rorty and His Critics* (Malden, MA, and Oxford: Blackwell, 2000), pp. 31–55.

77. See the footnote on p. 136 of 'Wahrheitstheorien'. The construction of the theory of validity goes back and forth between Dummett and practical discourses. Habermas used the former to generalize the case of epistemic validity to moral validity, whereas moral validity initially served as the model for understanding epistemic validity.

78. These three references are connected at the metatheoretical level in order to take account of our realist intuitions.

79. Habermas, 'Introduction: Realism after the Linguistic Turn', in *Truth and Justification*, pp. 1–50.

80. See Apel, *Transformation der Philosophie II*, pp. 358–435.

81. Habermas, *Legitimation Crisis*, pp. 102–10; Habermas, *Communication and the Evolution of Society*, trans. Thomas McCarthy (Boston, MA: Beacon Press, 1979), pp. 69–94.

82. Habermas, *Moral Consciousness and Communicative Action*, p. 93.

83. It should be recalled that the difficulties of such

a symmetry were raised by Thomas McCarthy as early as 1972.

84. Habermas, *Truth and Justification*, p. 190.

85. Here again, my point 1 below corresponds to sections (1)–(5) and my point 2 to sections (6)–(8) of Habermas's introduction.

86. Habermas, 'Discourse Ethics: Notes on a Program of Philosophical Justification', in Habermas, *Moral Consciousness and Communicative Action*, pp. 43–115.

87. Habermas, 'Morality and Ethical Life: Does Hegel's Critique of Kant Apply to Discourse Ethics?', in *Moral Consciousness and Communicative Action*, pp. 195–216.

88. Habermas, 'Morality, Society, and Ethics: An Interview with Torben Hviid Nielsen', in Habermas, *Justification and Application: Remarks on Discourse Ethics*, trans. Ciaran Cronin (Cambridge: Polity, 1995), pp. 147–76.

89. As we have seen, the reconstruction of moral-psychological development presupposes standardized conditions of socialization. Therefore, *additional hypotheses*, specifically sociological hypotheses, can explain how and why moral judgement and its development are susceptible to regressive pathologies, in particular pathologies bound up with identity (see I.B.2, I.C.2, II.A.3 above and II.D.2 below).

90. Habermas, 'Remarks on Discourse Ethics', in *Justification and Application*, pp. 19–112 and Habermas, 'A Genealogical Analysis of the Cognitive Content of Morality', in *The Inclusion of the Other*, pp. 3–48.

91. Habermas, 'On the Pragmatic, the Ethical, and the Moral Employment of Practical Reason', in *Justification and Application*, pp. 1–18.

92. Habermas, 'Rightness versus Truth: On the Sense

of Normative Validity in Moral Judgements and Norms', in *Truth and Justification*, pp. 237–76.

93. This is a response to an objection raised by Apel in *Auseinandersetzungen in Erprobung des transzendentalpragmatischen Ansatzes*, pp. 689–838, against Habermas's reformulation of the normativity of discourse required by the theory of law.

94. Habermas, 'On the Architectonics of Discursive Differentiation', in *Between Naturalism and Religion*, pp. 77–98.

95. In what follows, point 1 corresponds to sections (1)–(3), point 2 to sections (4) and (5), point 3 to sections (6)–(8), and point 4 to sections (9)–(11) of Habermas's introduction.

96. Habermas, 'Popular Sovereignty as Procedure' (1988), in *Between Facts and Norms*, pp. 463–90.

97. Habermas, 'Law and Morality', in *The Tanner Lectures on Human Values*, vol. 8, ed. Sterling M. McMurrin (Cambridge: Cambridge University Press, 1988), pp. 217–79.

98. According to Habermas, this deliberative solution was indicated by Julius Fröbel, *System der sozialen Politik* (Mannheim, 1847), which he cites several times in this article.

99. Habermas, 'Three Normative Models of Democracy', in Habermas, *The Inclusion of the Other*, trans. Ciaran Cronin (Cambridge: Polity, 2002), pp. 239–52.

100. Habermas, 'Political Communication in Media Society: Does Democracy Still Have an Epistemic Dimension? The Impact of Normative Theory on Empirical Research', in *Europe: The Faltering Project*, trans. Ciaran Cronin (Cambridge: Polity, 2008), pp. 138–83.

101. Habermas, 'On the Internal Relation between the Rule of Law and Democracy', in *The Inclusion of the Other*, pp. 253–64; Habermas, 'Constitutional

Democracy: A Paradoxical Union of Contradictory Principles?' (2001), in Habermas, *Time of Transitions*, trans. Ciaran Cronin and Max Pensky (Cambridge: Polity, 2006), pp. 113–28.

102. This is the psychological and intellectual effect of a learning process in stages where each successively higher stage relativizes the type of reasons defended at a lower stage.

103. Habermas, 'On the Relation between the Nation, the Rule of Law and Democracy', in *The Inclusion of the Other*, pp. 129–54. This question also touches on that of the role of historical discourse, caught between its contribution to the national narrative and its function in fostering critical distance from identities, a question addressed by Habermas in the context of his contributions to the historians' debate during the 1980s.

104. Habermas, 'Equal Treatment of Cultures and the Limits of Postmodern Liberalism', in *Between Naturalism and Religion*, pp. 271–311.

105. Here Habermas is referring to his article, 'Religion in the Public Sphere: Cognitive Presuppositions for the "Public Use of Reason" by Religious and Secular Citizens', in *Between Naturalism and Religion*, pp. 101–48.

106. Here Habermas is referring to his essay, 'Remarks on Legitimation through Human Rights', in *The Postnational Constellation*, pp. 113–29. For a revised version of his position, see: Habermas, 'Does the Constitutionalization of International Law Still Have a Chance?', in Habermas, *The Divided West*, trans. Ciaran Cronin (Cambridge: Polity, 2006), pp. 115–93; Habermas, 'The Constitutionalization of International Law and the Legitimation Problems of a Constitution for Society', in *Europe: The Faltering Project*, pp. 109–30.

107. Here, again, point 1 below corresponds to both

sections (1)–(4) and (5)–(7), point 2 to sections (8) and (9) and point 3 to sections (10)–(13) of Habermas's introduction.

108. Here Habermas is referring to his essay, 'Does Philosophy Still Have a Purpose?', in Habermas, *Philosophical-Political Profiles*, trans. Frederick G. Lawrence (London: Heinemann, 1981), pp. 1–20.

109. Habermas, 'Philosophy as Stand-In and Interpreter', in *Moral Consciousness and Communicative Action*, pp. 1–20; Habermas, 'What Theories Can Accomplish – And What They Can't', in Habermas, *The Past as Future*, trans. Max Pensky (Lincoln, NE: University of Nebraska Press, 1994), pp. 121–41; Habermas, 'The Relationship between Theory and Practice Revisited', in Habermas, *Truth and Justification*, pp. 277–92. Here we should note that, in this fifth introduction, Habermas fails to mention, with regard to this second retrospective article concerning his whole theoretical construction of the 1970s, something which nevertheless constituted its central axis – namely, the implications of these postmetaphysical coordinates for his own constructive puzzle strategy with the hermeneutical and heuristic role of the convergences between different theoretical fragments belonging to several disciplines and with the role that must nevertheless be played by normal argument ('Philosophy as Stand-In and Interpreter', pp. 14–15). This explains the original constructive structure of the major works such as *Theory of Communicative Action* and *Between Facts and Norms* as we have seen, and the elucidations and readjustments in the second stage of the organic growth of theory (see I.D.3 and 4).

110. Habermas, 'The Unity of Reason in the Diversity of Its Voices', in *Postmetaphysical Thinking*, pp. 115–48.

111. Here Habermas is referring to his essays, 'Metaphysics after Kant', in *Postmetaphysical Thinking*, pp. 10–27, and 'Themes in Postmetaphysical Thinking', in *Postmetaphysical Thinking*, pp. 28–53. I discussed the transformations of reason in the first part of this introduction.

112. See Edmund Husserl, *Ideas: General Introduction to Pure Phenomenology*, trans. W. R. Boyce Gibson (London and New York: Routledge, 2012 [1931]) and *The Crisis of European Sciences and Transcendental Phenomenology: An Introduction to Phenomenological Philosophy*, trans. David Carr (Evanston, IL: Northwestern University Press, 1970).

113. Habermas, 'From Worldviews to the Lifeworld', in Habermas, *Postmetaphysical Thinking II: Essays and Replies*, trans. Ciaran Cronin (Cambridge: Polity, 2017), pp. 3–27 and 'The Language Game of Responsible Agency and the Problem of Free Will', *Philosophical Explorations* 10/1 (2007): 13–50.

114. Habermas, 'The Boundary between Faith and Knowledge: On the Reception and Contemporary Importance of Kant's Philosophy of Religion', in *Between Naturalism and Religion*, pp. 209–47 and Habermas, 'Religion in the Public Sphere of "Post-Secular" Society', in Habermas, *Postmetaphysical Thinking II*.

115. Habermas, 'An Awareness of What is Missing', in Habermas, *An Awareness of What is Missing: Faith and Reason in a Post-Secular Age*, ed. Michael Reder and Josef Schmidt, trans. Ciaran Cronin (Cambridge: Polity, 2010), pp. 15–23.

116. Habermas, 'Transcendence from Within, Transcendence in this World', in Don S. Browning and Francis Schüssler Fiorenza (eds), *Habermas, Modernity, and Public Theology* (New York: Crossroad, 1992), pp. 226–50.

1. Foundations of Sociology in the Theory of Language

1. Jürgen Habermas, 'Reflections on the Linguistic Foundations of Sociology: The Christian Gauss Lectures (Princeton University, February–March, 1971)', in Habermas, *On the Pragmatics of Social Interaction*, trans. Barbara Fultner (Cambridge: Polity, 2001), pp. 1–103.
2. See the important habilitation thesis of K.-O. Apel, *Die Idee der Sprache in der Tradition des Humanismus von Dante bis Vico* (Bonn: Bouvier, 1963).
3. However, for criticism, see Habermas, 'On Hermeneutics' Claim to Universality' (1970), in Karl Mueller-Vollmer (ed.), *The Hermeneutics Reader* (New York: Continuum, 1985), pp. 294–319.
4. Habermas, *On the Logic of the Social Sciences*, trans. Shierry Weber Nicholsen and Jerry A. Stark (Cambridge: Polity, 1988).
5. Habermas, *Knowledge and Human Interests*, trans. Jeremy J. Shapiro (Cambridge: Polity, 1987); for a retrospective view on this work, see Habermas, 'Nach dreißig Jahren: Bemerkungen zu *Erkenntnis und Interesse*', in Stefan Müller-Doohm (ed.), *Das Interesse der Vernunft* (Frankfurt am Main: Suhrkamp, 2000), pp. 12–20, here pp. 17f.
6. Habermas, *The Structural Transformation of the Public Sphere: An Inquiry into a Category of Bourgeois Society*, trans. Thomas Burger and Frederick Lawrence (Cambridge: Polity, 1989); Habermas, *Toward a Rational Society*, Jeremy J. Shapiro (Cambridge: Polity, 1987).
7. Habermas, *Theory and Practice*, trans. John Viertel (Cambridge: Polity, 1988).
8. For an account of this early phase of my philosophi-

cal development that remains valid, see Thomas McCarthy, *The Critical Theory of Jürgen Habermas* (Cambridge, MA: MIT Press, 1978).

9. Hauke Brunkhorst, 'Paradigm-Core and Theory-Dynamics in Critical Social Theory: People and Programs', in *Philosophy and Social Criticism* 24/6 (1988): 67–110.

10. See my introduction to *Theory and Practice*.

11. Habermas, *On the Pragmatics of Social Interaction*, pp. 26f (translation amended).

12. For a more detailed account, see Habermas, *The Theory of Communicative Action*, trans. Thomas McCarthy, 2 vols (Boston, MA: Beacon Press, 1984, 1987), vol. 1, pp. 113–17.

13. See the notes for a seminar 'Vorbereitende Bemerkungen zur kommunikativen Kompetenz', reprinted in Jürgen Habermas and Niklas Luhmann, *Theorie der Gesellschaft oder Sozialtechnologie* (Frankfurt am Main: Suhrkamp, 1971), pp. 101–41.

14. John Searle, *Speech Acts* (Cambridge: Cambridge University Press, 1969).

15. Habermas, *On the Pragmatics of Social Interaction*, p. 74.

16. Habermas, *On the Pragmatics of Social Interaction*, p. 85.

17. Stephen Toulmin, *The Uses of Argument* (Cambridge: Cambridge University Press, 1964).

18. See the introduction to vol. 2 of the *Studienausgabe* (Chapter 2 in this volume).

19. I wrote my contribution to the Festschrift for Walter Schultz (Habermas, '**Wahrheitstheorien**', in Helmut Fahrenbach [ed.], *Wirklichkeit und Reflexion*, [Pfullingen: Neske, 1973], pp. 211–66) before moving to Starnberg and presented it in a seminar at Heidelberg in autumn 1971 at the invitation of Michael Theunissen.

20. In what follows I refer to the overview in 'Erläuterungen zum Begriff des kommunikativen Handelns' (1982), in Habermas, *Vorstudien und Ergänzungen zur Theorie des kommunikativen Handelns* (Frankfurt am Main: Suhrkamp, 1984), pp. 571–605.

21. Habermas, 'Actions, Speech Acts, Linguistically Mediated Interactions, and the Lifeworld', in Habermas, *On the Pragmatics of Communication*, ed. and trans. Maeve Cooke (Cambridge: Polity, 1988), pp. 215–56.

22. Searle, *Expression and Meaning* (Cambridge: Cambridge University Press, 1979), ch. 5.

23. For a more detailed account, see Habermas, *Theory of Communicative Action*, vol. 2, pp. 135–40.

24. On this, see *Theory of Communicative Action*, vol. 2, pp. 256–82.

25. On this, see *Theory of Communicative Action*, vol. 1, pp. 273–344.

26. Michael Theunissen, *The Other: Studies in the Social Ontology of Husserl, Heidegger, Sartre, and Buber*, trans. Christopher Macann (Cambridge, MA: MIT Press, 1984), pt. I.

27. 'Individuation through Socialization', in Habermas, *Postmetaphysical Thinking*, trans. William Mark Hohengarten (Cambridge: Polity, 1992), pp. 149–204.

28. Habermas, 'Reflections on Communicative Pathology', in *On the Pragmatics of Social Interaction*, pp. 129–70.

29. Habermas, 'Aspects of the Rationality of Action', in Theodor F. Geraets (ed.), *Rationality Today* (Ottawa: University of Ottawa Press, 1979), pp. 185–204.

30. *Theory of Communicative Action*, vol. 2, pp. 312–18. See Hauke Brunkhorst, *Habermas* (Leipzig:

Reklam, 2006), p. 88, with an ironic allusion to Gehlen: 'There are not only primitive human beings in the cellar and advanced culture on the roof; in between there are also forms of social life whose evolution is a function in equal parts of blind random variation and of moral-cognitive learning processes whose selective consequences must then be stabilized by institutions.'

31. *Theory of Communicative Action*, vol. 2, pp. 318–31.
32. Habermas, *Communication and the Evolution of Society*, trans. Thomas McCarthy (Cambridge: Polity, 1984), pp. 95–177.
33. Habermas, 'Was macht eine Lebensform rational?' in *Erläuterungen zur Diskursethik* (Frankfurt am Main: Suhrkamp, 1991), pp. 31–48.
34. Habermas, 'Reflections on Communicative Pathology', in *On the Pragmatics of Social Interaction*, pp. 129–70.
35. Wolfgang Schluchter, *Die Entwicklung des okzidentalen Rationalismus: Eine Analyse von Max Webers Gesellschaftsgeschichte* (Tübingen: Mohr Siebeck, 1979).
36. See also Klaus Eder, *Die Entstehung staatlich organisierter Gesellschaften* (Frankfurt am Main: Suhrkamp, 1976).
37. On 'reconstructive functionalism', see Bernhard Peters, *Die Integration moderner Gesellschaften* (Frankfurt am Main: Suhrkamp, 1993), pp. 396ff.
38. Habermas, 'Reconstruction and Interpretation in the Social Sciences', in *Moral Consciousness and Communicative Action*, trans. Christian Lenhardt and Shierry Weber Nicholsen (Cambridge: Polity, 1990), pp. 21–42; see also: 'Philosophy as Stand-In and Interpreter', ibid., pp. 1–20.
39. Habermas, 'Conceptions of Modernity: A Look Back at Two Traditions', in *The Postnational*

Constellation, ed. and trans. Max Pensky (Cambridge: Polity, 2001), pp. 130–56.

40. Habermas, The Philosophical Discourse of Modernity: Twelve Lectures, trans. Frederick G. Lawrence (Cambridge: Polity, 1987), pp. 106–30.

41. Axel Honneth, 'Verflüssigung des Sozialen', Neue Zeitschrift für Sozialforschung 2 (2008): 84: 'One could easily get the impression that recent sociology … has turned its back irrevocably on the generation of its founding fathers; from Weber and Durkheim to Talcott Parsons, by contrast, it was taken for granted that an adequate basic conception of the social world could be developed only by using concepts, models or assumptions of moral theory.'

42. See the excellent account of this transition in Herbert Marcuse, Reason and Revolution (Boston, MA: Beacon Press, 1960).

43. An exception was France during the 1960s, though there structuralist anthropology took over this role from sociology only on a temporary basis.

44. This does not exclude committed accounts such as that of Hans Joas and Wolfgang Knöbl in Sozialtheorie: Zwanzig einführende Vorlesungen (Frankfurt am Main: Suhrkamp, 2004).

45. For a recent survey, see Simon Susen, The 'Postmodern Turn' in the Social Sciences (New York: Palgrave Macmillan, 2015).

2. Theory of Rationality and Theory of Meaning

1. See the introduction to vol. 1 of the Studienausgabe (chapter 1 in this volume).

2. Jürgen Habermas, 'What is Universal Pragmatics?', in Habermas, On the Pragmatics of Communication, ed. and trans. Maeve Cooke (Cambridge: Polity, 1988), pp. 21–104.

3. The cooperation with Ernst Tugendhat, who wrote his book *Vorlesungen zur Einführung in die sprachanalytische Philosophie* (Frankfurt am Main: Suhrkamp, 1976; English translation: *Traditional and Analytical Philosophy: Lectures on the Philosophy of Language* [Cambridge: Cambridge University Press, 1982]) at the Max Planck Institute in Starnberg, had of course already given rise to intensive discussions of issues in the theory of language.

4. Habermas, 'Hermeneutic and Analytic Philosophy: Two Complementary Versions of the Linguistic Turn', in Habermas, *Truth and Justification*, trans. Barbara Fultner (Cambridge: Polity, 2003), pp. 51–82.

5. Habermas, 'Toward a Critique of the Theory of Meaning', in Habermas, *Postmetaphysical Thinking*, trans. William Mark Hohengarten (Cambridge: Polity, 1992), pp. 57–87.

6. Habermas, 'Peirce and Communication', in Habermas, *Postmetaphysical Thinking*, pp. 88–114.

7. Karl-Otto Apel, 'Sprache und Wahrheit in der gegenwärtigen Situation der Philosophie' (1959), in Apel, *Transformation der Philosophie*, vol. I (Frankfurt am Main: Suhrkamp, 1973), pp. 138–66.

8. Albrecht Wellmer, *Methodologie als Erkenntnistheorie: Zur Wissenschaftslehre Karl R. Poppers* (Frankfurt am Main: Suhrkamp, 1967).

9. Apel, *Transformation der Philosophie*, pp. 225–75.

10. It was only later that I dealt with Donald Davidson's prominent theory of truth, to which Richard Rorty had already drawn my attention in 1971; see Habermas, *Truth and Justification*, pp. 112–21.

11. For criticism of Searle's intentionalist conception of language, see Habermas, 'Comments on John Searle's "Meaning, Communication,

and Representation"', in *On the Pragmatics of Communication*, pp. 257–76.

12. See Robert B. Brandom, *Making it Explicit: Reasoning, Representing, and Discursive Commitment* (Cambridge, MA: Harvard University Press, 1994).

13. Habermas, **'Some Further Clarifications of the Concept of Communicative Rationality'** (1996), in *On the Pragmatics of Communication*, pp. 307–42.

14. From an evolutionary perspective, the shared life-world of small kinship groups is at the same time the product of, and provides in turn the background for, two complementary forms of communication: *ordinary language* meets functional imperatives in everyday cooperation, whereas *ritual communication* gives rise to normative obligations. A partial overlap or merger may explain the illocutionary meaning spectrum of normative obligations in ordinary language. See Habermas, *Postmetaphysical Thinking II*, trans. Ciaran Cronin (Cambridge: Polity, 2017), 'Linguistification of the Sacred: In Place of a Preface', pp. vii–xv, and chs 2 and 3.

15. Habermas, **'From Kant's "Ideas" of Pure Reason to the "Idealizing" Presuppositions of Communicative Action: Reflections on the Detranscendentalized "Use of Reason"'**, in William Rehg and James Bohman (eds), *Pluralism and the Pragmatic Turn: The Transformation of Critical Theory, Essays in Honor of Thomas McCarthy* (Cambridge, MA: MIT Press, 2001), pp. 11–40.

16. When the text was reprinted ten years later, I only added a couple of footnotes: Habermas, **'Wahrheitstheorien'**, in Habermas, *Vorstudien und Ergänzungen zur Theorie des kommunikativen Handelns* (Frankfurt am Main: Suhrkamp, 1984), pp. 127–86.

17. See also my commemorative speech '"... And to

Define America, Her Athletic Democracy": In memory of Richard Rorty', in Habermas, *Europe: The Faltering Project*, trans. Ciaran Cronin (Cambridge: Polity, 2008), pp. 3–16.

18. Habermas, **'Richard Rorty's Pragmatic Turn'**, in Brandom (ed.), *Rorty and His Critics* (Malden, MA, and Oxford: Blackwell, 2000), pp. 31–55.

19. Stephen Toulmin, *The Uses of Argument* (Cambridge: Cambridge University Press, 1964).

20. Habermas, **'Wahrheitstheorien'**, p. 144.

21. **'Introduction: Realism after the Linguistic Turn'**, in Habermas, *Truth and Justification*, pp. 1–50.

22. Hilary Putnam, *Realism and Reason: Philosophical Papers Volume 3* (Cambridge: Cambridge University Press, 1983). But see my critique of Putnam's Aristotelianism in practical philosophy: Habermas, 'Norms and Values: On Hilary Putnam's Kantian Pragmatism', in Habermas, *Truth and Justification*, trans. Barbara Fultner (Cambridge: Polity, 2003), pp. 213–35.

3. Discourse Ethics

1. Manfred Riedel, *Rehabilitierung der praktischen Philosophie, Band II: Rezeption, Argumentation, Diskussion* (Freiburg: Rombach, 1974).

2. Paul Lorenzen, *Normative Logic and Ethics* (Mannheim: Bibliographisches Institut, 1969); Lorenzen and Oswald Schwemmer (eds), *Konstruktive Ethik und Wissenschaftstheorie* (Mannheim: Bibliographisches Institut, 1973); Karl-Otto Apel, 'The *a priori* of the Communication Community and the Foundation of Ethics: The Problem of a Rational Foundation of Ethics in the Scientific Age', in Apel, *Towards a Transformation of Philosophy*, trans. Glyn Adey and David Frisby

(London: Routledge & Kegan Paul, 1980), pp. 225–300.

3. Jürgen Habermas, 'Dogmatism, Reason and Decision: On Theory and Practice in Our Scientific Civilization' (1963), in Habermas, *Theory and Practice*, trans. John Viertel (Cambridge: Polity, 1988), pp. 253–82.

4. Habermas, 'Technology and Science as "Ideology"' (1968), in Habermas, *Toward a Rational Society*, trans. Jeremy J. Shapiro (Cambridge: Polity, 1987), pp. 81–122.

5. Habermas, 'The Analytical Theory of Science and Dialectics' (1963), in Theodor W. Adorno et al. (eds), *The Positivist Dispute in German Sociology*, trans. Glyn Adey and David Frisby (London: Heinemann, 1976), pp. 131–62; Habermas, 'Wertfreiheit und Objektivität', in Otto Stammer (ed.), *Max Weber und die Soziologie heute* (Tübingen: Mohr Siebeck, 1965), pp. 74–81; Habermas, *On the Logic of the Social Sciences*, trans. Shierry Weber Nicholsen and Jerry A. Stark (Cambridge: Polity, 1988).

6. Habermas, *Knowledge and Human Interests*, trans. Jeremy J. Shapiro (Cambridge: Polity, 1987).

7. Habermas, *Legitimation Crisis*, trans. Thomas McCarthy (Cambridge: Polity, 1988), pp. 102–16 (the original German edition was published in 1973, two years after John Rawls's *A Theory of Justice* which I did not read until it was translated into German in 1975).

8. Habermas, *The Theory of Communicative Action*, trans. Thomas McCarthy, 2 vols (Boston, MA: Beacon Press, 1984, 1987), vol. 2, pp. 43–76.

9. Habermas, *Legitimation Crisis*, pp. 107f.

10. Habermas, *Legitimation Crisis*, p. 108.

11. Habermas, *Legitimation Crisis*, p. 110.

12. Kohlberg's theory inspired above all the research of

Rainer Döbert, Klaus Eder and Gertrud Nunner-Winkler. See also Habermas, 'Moral Development and Ego Identity', in Habermas, *Communication and the Evolution of Society*, trans. Thomas McCarthy (Cambridge: Polity, 1984), pp. 69–94.

13. Habermas, *Moral Consciousness and Communicative Action*, trans. Christian Lenhardt and Shierry Weber Nicholsen (Cambridge: Polity, 1990), pp. 116–94.

14. The climate in social psychology is more sympathetic towards Kohlberg's theoretical approach; see Gertrud Nunner-Winkler, 'Ethik der freiwilligen Selbstbindung', in *Erwägen-Wissen-Ethik*, 4 (2003): 579–89; Nunner-Winkler, Marion Meyer-Nikele, and Doris Wohlrab, *Integration durch Moral: Moralische Motivation und Ziviltugenden Jugendlicher* (Wiesbaden: VS Verlag für Sozialwissenschaften, 2006).

15. See Habermas, 'Lawrence Kohlberg and Neo-Aristotelianism', in Habermas, *Justification and Application: Remarks on Discourse Ethics*, trans. by Ciaran Cronin (Cambridge: Polity, 1995), pp. 113–32.

16. Habermas, 'Discourse Ethics: Notes on a Program of Philosophical Justification', in *Moral Consciousness and Communicative Action*, pp. 43–115.

17. See Lutz Wingert, *Gemeinsinn und Moral* (Frankfurt am Main: Suhrkamp, 1993).

18. Like John Rawls in his Dewey Lectures ('Kantian Constructivism', *Journal of Philosophy* 77 [1980]: 515–72), although I was not familiar with them at the time, my approach is also a 'Kantian constructivist' one.

19. Habermas, *Moral Consciousness and Communicative Action*, pp. 66, 65.

20. Habermas, 'Morality and Ethical Life: Does Hegel's Critique of Kant Apply to Discourse Ethics?', in

Moral Consciousness and Communicative Action, pp. 195–216.

21. Habermas, 'Morality, Society, and Ethics: An Interview with Torben Hviid Nielsen', in *Justification and Application*, pp. 147–76.

22. Axel Honneth, *The Struggle for Recognition*, trans. Joel Anderson (Cambridge, MA: MIT Press, 1996). Honneth (ed.), *Pathologien des Sozialen: Die Aufgaben der Sozialphilosophie* (Frankfurt am Main: Fischer, 1994); Mattias Iser, *Empörung und Fortschritt: Grundlagen einer kritischen Theorie der Gesellschaft* (Frankfurt am Main: Campus, 2008).

23. Habermas, 'Remarks on Discourse Ethics', in *Justification and Application*, pp. 19–112.

24. Klaus Günther, *The Sense of Appropriateness: Application Discourses in Morality and Law*, trans. John Farrell (Albany, NY: SUNY Press, 1993).

25. In *Journal of Philosophy*, 92, 3 (1995).

26. John Rawls, 'Kantian Constructivism in Moral Theory', in Rawls, *Collected Papers*, ed. Samuel Freeman (Cambridge, MA: Harvard University Press, 1999), pp. 303–58.

27. See my reflections on the debate in James Gordon Finlayson and Fabian Freyenhagen (eds), *Habermas and Rawls: Disputing the Political* (New York: Routledge, 2011), pp. 283–304.

28. Habermas, '"Reasonable" versus "True", or the Morality of Worldviews', in Habermas, *The Inclusion of the Other*, trans. Ciaran Cronin (Cambridge: Polity, 2002), pp. 75–101.

29. Habermas, 'A Genealogical Analysis of the Cognitive Content of Morality', in *The Inclusion of the Other*, pp. 3–48.

30. Habermas, 'On the Pragmatic, the Ethical, and the Moral Employment of Practical Reason' in *Justification and Application*, pp. 1–18.

31. Mattias Vogel and Lutz Wingert (eds), *Wissen zwischen Entdeckung und Konstruktion: Erkenntnistheoretische Kontroversen* (Frankfurt am Main: Suhrkamp, 2003) (with contributions by Wolfgang Detel, Ian Hacking, Thomas Nagel and Hilary Putnam, among others).

32. Habermas, **'Rightness versus Truth: On the Sense of Normative Validity in Moral Judgements and Norms'** in Habermas, *Truth and Justification*, trans. Barbara Fultner (Cambridge: Polity, 2003), pp. 237–76.

33. Habermas, *The Future of Human Nature*, trans. Hannah Beister, Max Pensky and William Rehg (Cambridge: Polity, 2003).

34. Habermas, *Between Facts and Norms*, trans. William Rehg (Cambridge: Polity, 1996).

35. Habermas, **'On the Architectonics of Discursive Differentiation'**, in Habermas, *Between Naturalism and Religion*, trans. Ciaran Cronin (Cambridge: Polity, 2008), pp. 77–98.

4. Political Theory

1. [From the 1960s onwards, Habermas has published his essays on political issues aimed at a broader, not primarily academic, public in a series entitled 'Kleine politische Schriften', of which 12 volumes have appeared to date. Many of these collections have appeared in English translation under individual titles, most recently *The Lure of Technocracy* (= vol. XII of the 'short political writings'). *Trans.*]

2. Jürgen Habermas, *The Structural Transformation of the Public Sphere: An Inquiry into a Category of Bourgeois Society*, trans. Thomas Burger and Frederick Lawrence (Cambridge: Polity, 1992) (originally published in German in 1962).

3. The method of rational reconstruction explained in the first introduction meets with widespread incomprehension in sociology, whereas, interestingly enough, it receives a sympathetic response in political science: see Daniel Gaus, *Der Sinn von Demokratie* (Frankfurt am Main: Campus, 2009), pp. 222–34; for a more recent account, see Gaus, 'Rational Reconstruction as a Method of Political Theory between Social Critique and Empirical Social Science', *Constellations* 20/4 (2013): 553–70; also Markus Patberg, 'Suprastaatliche Verfassungspolitik und die Methode der rationalen Rekonstruktion', *Zeitschrift für Politische Theorie* 53/3 (2014): 80–98.

4. In the theoretical introduction to the empirical study Habermas et al., *Student und Politik* (Neuwied: Luchterhand, 1961) and in *Structural Transformation of the Public Sphere*, I refer to the works of the Austro-Marxist Karl Renner and the Keynesian John Stratchey, among others, and to the famous controversy between Wolfgang Abendroth and Ernst Forsthoff at the annual meeting of the German association of teachers of constitutional law (Vereinigung der Deutschen Staatsrechtslehrer) in 1952.

5. Professors such as Ernst Forsthoff and Werner Weber belonged to the liberal-conservative 'centre of society' not only as academics, but also within the political spectrum of the early Federal Republic. See Ernst Forsthoff and Carl Schmitt, *Briefwechsel 1926–1974* (Berlin: Akademie Verlag, 2007). The Schmittian school systematically and carefully recruited young talent to train a new generation of legal experts. The Ebracher Sommerkursen lent the ostracized Carl Schmitt the aura of the leader of a secret sect. See Dirk van Laak, *Gespräche in der Sicherheit des Schweigens: Carl Schmitt*

in der politischen Geistesgeschichte der frühen Bundesrepublik (Berlin: De Gruyter, 1993).

6. I used this formula in a review of Reinhart Koselleck's dissertation *Kritik und Krise* in *Merkur* 5 (1960): 468–77. There I argued with reference to the discussion of the French Enlightenment:

> According to its own idea, the public character of political decisions was supposed to make it possible to invert the (Hobbesian) principle *auctoritas non veritas facit legem* – namely, to bring the activity of the state into agreement with the interest of the nation – de facto with the interest of the bourgeois class – through reasoned public discussion. The intention was not to moralize politics as such, but to rationalize it by means of the principle of publicity. ... At the same time, this intention, however much it functioned as an ideology, involved the idea that political authority would be dissolved into rational authority in the medium of such a public sphere and that rule would undergo a global transformation. (p. 472)

7. Habermas, *Toward a Rational Society*, trans. Jeremy J. Shapiro (Cambridge: Polity, 1987).
8. Niklas Luhmann, *Zweckbegriff und Systemrationalität* (Tübingen: Mohr Siebeck, 1968). Luhmann developed a much more differentiated account of his political theory in Luhmann, *Political Theory in the Welfare State*, trans. John Bednarz, Jr (Berlin, New York: W. de Gruyter, 1990), and Luhmann, *Die Politik der Gesellschaft* (Frankfurt am Main: Suhrkamp, 2000).
9. For criticism of the decisionistic and technocratic model, see Habermas, 'Verwissenschaftlichte Politik und öffentliche Meinung', in Habermas, *Technik und Wissenschaft als 'Ideologie'* (Frankfurt am Main: Suhrkamp, 1968), pp. 120–45.

10. Habermas, *Toward a Rational Society*, pp. 65ff. and 74ff.

11. Habermas, 'Law and Morality' (1986), in Sterling M. McMurrin (ed.), *The Tanner Lectures on Human Values VIII* (Salt Lake City, UT: University of Utah Press, 1988), pp. 217–80.

12. See the preface to Habermas, *Between Facts and Norms: Contributions to a Discourse Theory of Law and Democracy*, trans. William Rehg (Cambridge: Polity, 1996).

13. In fact, the theme of the development of the European Union, to which I have returned repeatedly, also belongs in this context. In various essays on this topic, I have tried as best I can to keep up with the extensive empirical literature; however, my analysis is so closely interwoven with my committed stances on contemporary issues that I must leave the discussion of the European theme to one side. See Habermas, 'Does Europe Need a Constitution? Response to Dieter Grimm' (1995), in Habermas, *The Inclusion of the Other*, trans. Ciaran Cronin (Cambridge: Polity, 1998), pp. 155–64; Habermas, *The Divided West* (2004), trans. Ciaran Cronin (Cambridge: Polity, 2006), Part II; Habermas, *Europe: The Faltering Project* (2008), trans. Ciaran Cronin (Cambridge: Polity, 2009); Habermas, *The Crisis of the European Union* (2011), trans. Ciaran Cronin (Cambridge: Polity, 2012); and Habermas, *The Lure of Technocracy* (2013), trans. Ciaran Cronin (Cambridge: Polity, 2015).

The corresponding texts were originally published in volumes of the *Kleine politische Schriften* series: Habermas, *Die Zeit der Übergänge* (Frankfurt am Main: Suhrkamp, 2001) (specifically the essays: 'Euroskepsis, Markteuropa oder Europa der (Welt) Bürger' and 'Braucht Europa eine Verfassung?'); Habermas, *Der gespaltene Westen* (Frankfurt am

Main: Suhrkamp, 2004) (specifically: 'Der 15. Februar – oder: Was die Europäer verbindet' and 'Ist die Herausbildung einer europäischen Identität nötig, und ist sie möglich?'); Habermas, *Ach, Europa* (Frankfurt am Main: Suhrkamp, 2008) (specifically: 'Europa und seine Immigranten' and 'Europapolitik in der Sackgasse').

14. Habermas, 'Popular Sovereignty as Procedure' (1988), in *Between Facts and Norms*, pp. 463–90.

15. Habermas, 'Three Normative Models of Democracy', in *The Inclusion of the Other*, pp. 239–52.

16. Habermas, 'Political Communication in Media Society: Does Democracy Still Have an Epistemic Dimension? The Impact of Normative Theory on Empirical Research', in *Europe: The Faltering Project*, pp. 138–83.

17. Habermas, *Between Facts and Norms*, pp. 133–67.

18. Habermas, 'On the Internal Relation between the Rule of Law and Democracy', in *The Inclusion of the Other*, pp. 253–64.

19. Cristina Lafont, 'Is the Ideal of a Deliberative Democracy Coherent?' in Samatha Besson and José Luis Marti (eds), *Deliberative Democracy and Its Discontents* (Aldershot: Ashgate, 2006), pp. 3–26. See my critique of mistaken expertocratic models of deliberative politics in: Habermas, 'Kommunikative Rationalität und grenzüberschreitende Politik: eine Replik', in Peter Niesen and Benjamin Herborth (eds), *Anarchie der kommunikativen Freiheit* (Frankfurt am Main: Suhrkamp, 2007), pp. 406–59, here pp. 435ff.

20. Habermas, 'Constitutional Democracy: A Paradoxical Union of Contradictory Principles?' (2001), in Habermas, *Time of Transitions*, trans. Ciaran Cronin and Max Pensky (Cambridge: Polity, 2006), pp. 113–28.

21. See Christopher F. Zurn, *Deliberative Democracy and the Institution of Judicial Review* (Cambridge: Cambridge University Press, 2007).

22. Habermas, 'Prepolitical Foundations of the Constitutional State?' in Habermas, *Between Naturalism and Religion*, trans. Ciaran Cronin (Cambridge: Polity, 2008), pp. 101–13.

23. Habermas, '**On the Relation between the Nation, the Rule of Law and Democracy**', in *The Inclusion of the Other*, pp. 129–54.

24. Habermas, '**Equal Treatment of Cultures and the Limits of Postmodern Liberalism**', in *Between Naturalism and Religion*, pp. 271–311.

25. See also my debate with Charles Taylor in Habermas, 'Struggles for Recognition in the Democratic Constitutional State', in *The Inclusion of the Other*, pp. 203–36.

26. Habermas, '**Religion in the Public Sphere: Cognitive Presuppositions for the "Public Use of Reason" by Religious and Secular Citizens**', in *Between Naturalism and Religion*, pp. 101–48.

27. Habermas, *The Past as Future* (1990), trans. Max Pensky (Lincoln, NE: University of Nebraska Press, 1994).

28. Habermas, *The Past as Future*, p. 77: 'With the deconstruction of bipolar tensions it's becoming increasingly clear that the one remaining super-power has really very few conflicts under control. The developing disparities in the global economy, the failures of the World Bank's programs, the uncontrolled spread of nuclear weapons, the emigration pressures from the mobile popula-tions of underdeveloped countries who have been uprooted from their traditional cultures, all come together to form a mixture as explosive as it is unpredictable. It demands a more broadly effec-tive network of global planning, as well as a

more neutral and efficient international policing force.'

29. Habermas, *The Past as Future*, pp. 9–24.

30. Habermas, *The Past as Future*, pp. 73ff.

31. Habermas, 'Kant's Idea of Perpetual Peace: At Two Hundred Years' Historical Remove', in *The Inclusion of the Other*, pp. 165–202. Habermas, 'The Postnational Constellation and the Future of Democracy', in *The Postnational Constellation: Political Essays*, ed. and trans. Max Pensky (Cambridge: Polity, 2001), pp. 58–112.

32. Habermas, *The Past as Future*, p. 20

33. Habermas, '**Remarks on Legitimation through Human Rights**', in *The Postnational Constellation*, pp. 113–29.

34. Habermas, '**Does the Constitutionalization of International Law Still Have a Chance?**', in *The Divided West*, pp. 115–93.

35. Habermas, '**A Political Constitution for the Pluralist World Society?**', in *Between Naturalism and Religion*, pp. 312–52. I dropped the reservation expressed by the question mark, which is still a feature of this outline, when I clarified it further in connection with questions of the European constitution: see section III of the essay on the constitution for Europe in *The Crisis of the European Union*, pp. 53–70.

36. In the meantime, I have developed this idea in Habermas, 'Zur Prinzipienkonkurrenz von Bürgergleichheit und Staatengleichheit im supranationalen Gemeinwesen', in *Der Staat*, 53/2 (2014): 167–92.

5. Critique of Reason

1. Ludger Honnefelder, *Woher kommen wir? Ursprünge der Moderne im Denken des Mittelalters* (Berlin: Berlin University Press, 2007).
2. In the introduction to his edited collection *Habermas: A Critical Reader* (Oxford and Malden, MA: Blackwell, 1999), pp. 1–28, Peter Dews offers a knowledgeable account of my metaphilosophical reflections in which he speaks of the 'avoidance of ultimate questions' (p. 20).
3. See Habermas, 'Literaturbericht zur philosophischen Diskussion um Marx und den Marxismus', *Philosophische Rundschau*, V/3–4 (1957): 165–235.
4. Habermas, 'Introduction: Some Difficulties in the Attempt to Link Theory and Practice', in Habermas, *Theory and Practice*, trans. John Viertel (London: Heinemann, 1974), p. 2 (translation amended).
5. For this criticism of my own position, see also Habermas, 'Nach dreißig Jahren: Bemerkungen zu *Erkenntnis und Interesse*', in Stefan Müller-Doohm (ed.), *Das Interesse der Vernunft* (Frankfurt am Main: Suhrkamp, 2000), pp. 12–22.
6. Habermas, *Theory and Practice*, p. 24.
7. I have reservations about using the now established term 'metaphilosophical'. The difference between language levels suggested by this expression does not adequately reflect the self-referential character of the critique of reason.
8. Habermas, '**Does Philosophy Still Have a Purpose?**', in Habermas, *Philosophical-Political Profiles*, trans. Frederick G. Lawrence (London: Heinemann, 1981), pp. 1–20.
9. Habermas, '**Philosophy as Stand-In and Interpreter**', in Habermas, *Moral Consciousness and*

Communicative Action, trans. Christian Lenhardt and Shierry Weber Nicholsen (Cambridge: Polity, 1992), pp. 1–20.

10. Habermas, 'Edmund Husserl über Lebenswelt, Philosophie und Wissenschaft', in Habermas, *Texte und Kontexte* (Frankfurt am Main: Suhrkamp, 1991), pp. 34–48.

11. On the question of civil disobedience, see Habermas, 'Civil Disobedience: Litmus Test for the Democratic Constitutional State', *Berkeley Journal of Sociology* 30 (1985): 95–116.

12. Habermas, 'What Theories Can Accomplish – And What They Can't', in Habermas, *The Past as Future*, trans. Max Pensky (Lincoln, NE: University of Nebraska Press, 1994), pp. 121–41.

13. Habermas, 'The Relationship between Theory and Practice Revisited', in Habermas, *Truth and Justification*, trans. Barbara Fultner (Cambridge: Polity, 2003), pp. 277–92, here p. 283.

14. Habermas, 'The Unity of Reason in the Diversity of Its Voices', in Habermas, *Postmetaphysical Thinking*, trans. William Mark Hohengarten (Cambridge: Polity, 1992), pp. 115–48.

15. Dieter Henrich, 'What is Metaphysics – What is Modernity? Twelve Theses against Jürgen Habermas', in Peter Dewes (ed.), *Habermas: A Critical Reader* (Oxford and Malden, MA: Blackwell, 1999), pp. 291–319. On the continuation of this discussion see, more recently, Dieter Henrich, *Denken und Selbstsein* (Frankfurt am Main: Suhrkamp, 2007), ch. IV.

16. Habermas, 'Metaphysics after Kant', in *Postmetaphysical Thinking*, pp. 10–27.

17. Habermas, 'Themes in Postmetaphysical Thinking', in *Postmetaphysical Thinking*, pp. 28–53; see also: Habermas, 'From Kant to Hegel and Back Again:

The Move toward Detranscendentalization', in *Truth and Justification*, pp. 131–74.

18. Habermas, 'From Worldviews to the Lifeworld', in Habermas, *Postmetaphysical Thinking II*, trans. Ciaran Cronin (Cambridge: Polity, 2017), pp. 3–27.

19. For the English version, see n. 20 below.

20. In Schelling's philosophy of nature, this role is played by the idealist concept of formation [*Bildung*], whereas Jean Piaget in his late work attempted to generalize the cognitive concept of learning tested in genetic structuralism in such a way that it is also suitable for naturalistic use in the biological sciences. Habermas, 'The Language Game of Responsible Agency and the Problem of Free Will', *Philosophical Explorations* 10/1 (2007): 13–50.

21. Habermas, 'The Boundary between Faith and Knowledge: On the Reception and Contemporary Importance of Kant's Philosophy of Religion', in Habermas, *Between Naturalism and Religion*, trans. Ciaran Cronin (Cambridge: Polity, 2008), pp. 209–47.

22. See Habermas, 'Religion in the Public Sphere of "Post-Secular" Society', in Habermas *Postmetaphysical Thinking II: Essays and Replies*, trans. Ciaran Cronin (Cambridge: Polity, 2017), pp. 210–24.

23. Habermas, 'An Awareness of What is Missing', in Habermas, *An Awareness of What is Missing: Faith and Reason in a Post-Secular Age*, ed. Michael Reder and Josef Schmidt, trans. Ciaran Cronin (Cambridge: Polity, 2010), pp. 15–23.

24. Don S. Browning and Schüssler Fiorenza (eds), *Habermas, Modernity, and Public Theology* (New York: Crossroad, 1992).

25. Such a change of heart was attributed to me in the media following my acceptance speech on receiving the German Peace Prize; see Habermas, 'Faith and

Knowledge', in Habermas, *The Future of Human Nature*, trans. Hannah Beister, Max Pensky and William Rehg (Cambridge: Polity, 2003), pp. 101–15.

26. Merlin Donald, *Origins of the Modern Mind: Three Stages in the Evolution of Culture and Cognition* (Cambridge, MA: Harvard University Press, 1991).

Index

Abendroth, Wolfgang 13, 202n.4
Adaptation, Goals, Integration
     and Latency (AGIL) 15, 20,
     21, 23, 50
Adler, Max 62
Adorno, Theodor 7, 8, 9, 11, 12,
     33, 34, 111, 151
   Critical Theory 126
   critique of reason 79
   Dialectic of Enlightenment 5
   dialectic of reason 34
   surplus value 61
American communitarianism 7
American neo-conservatism 7,
     25, 55
American pragmatism 6, 71
anthropology 77
   conservative anthropology 49
   cultural anthropology 149
   of knowledge interests 18
   philosophical anthropology 4,
     5, 9, 18
Apel, Kurt-Otto 4, 5–6, 7, 8–9,
     10, 12, 14, 36, 39, 43, 48,
     55, 60, 61, 65, 81, 83, 97,
     98, 159
   discourse ethics 105, 121
   transcendental pragmatics 82,
     100, 107
Arendt, Hannah 7

argumentation 21, 41, 43, 57, 98,
     101, 146
   communicative rationality
     94–5, 97
   discourse ethics 106–7, 116–17,
     119
   validity claims 87–8
Aristotle 7, 43, 47, 122, 128, 159
Austin, J.L. 66, 95
Austro-Marxism 176n.25, 202n.4
autonomy
   public and private 53, 55, 128,
     136–7, 150
Axial Age 141, 161

Benjamin, Walter 7, 8, 151
Between Facts and Norms 20, 50,
     52, 129, 131, 136, 142
Bildungshumanismus 159
Bismarck, Otto von 177n.27
Brandom, Robert 39, 64, 94, 97
Bühler, Karl 84, 183n.69
Bultmann, Rudolf 169

Carnap, Rudolf 81, 82
catch-up revolution 11
Chomsky, Noam 8, 17, 34, 66, 79
Christian Gauss Lectures 17, 19,
     31, 32, 39, 40, 60, 62, 65,
     68, 69, 95

citizenship 51, 138, 139
civil society 53, 130, 140
    industrial society 128
    political communication 134
    public sphere 126, 132
    state and 125
Cold War 6
colonialism 140
colonization of lifeworld 33,
    49–50, 73
common good 76, 102, 138
communicative action 65–6, 67,
    75–6
    evolution and 22
    formal pragmatics 69, 92
    lifeworld and 68, 69, 70, 73,
        160–3
    meaning of 67
    pragmatic concept of 67, 69
    see also speech acts
communicative competence 20,
    21, 31, 43, 66
    see also interactive competence
communicative rationality 33–4,
    37–8, 72, 86–94, 111
complementary hypotheses 23,
    24, 52
consensus 32, 48, 103, 112, 113
consensus theory of truth 18, 67,
    95, 96–7, 98
conservatism 7, 8
constitutional democracy 129,
    130
constitutional law 77, 125, 127,
    137
constitutional principles 138, 156
constitutional state 53, 128,
    135–7, 155
    nation, culture and religion
        137–41
    public interest and 126, 130
correspondence theory of truth
    35, 40–2, 79, 95
critical social theory 76, 79, 80,
    125, 155

Critical Theory 9, 25, 27, 28, 44,
    46, 57, 79, 126

Darwin, Charles 158
Davidson, Donald 39, 81, 94, 98
democracy 13, 51–3, 129–34
    citizenship 51, 138, 139
    communicative power 132
    constitutional democracy 129,
        130
    deliberative democracy 49, 51,
        52, 132–4
    inclusive democracy 49
    liberal models 52, 133
    origins of bourgeois democracy
        127
    philosophy and 155–6
    popular sovereignty 53, 131,
        133–4, 136
    public and private autonomy
        53, 55, 128, 136–7
    re-education and 11–12
    republican models 52, 133
    self-determination 53, 54, 139,
        141
denazification 122–3
    see also re-education
depoliticization 11, 13, 14
Derrida, Jacques 10
detranscendentalization 9, 11, 25,
    30, 34, 36–7, 39, 55–9
    communicative action 92–3
    language games 82–3
    postmetaphysical thinking 156,
        158–9, 162
    sociology 61, 84
Dewey, John 8, 129
dialectic
    of enlightenment 72
    of modernity 24, 33
    of the public sphere 19, 23–4,
        35
    of reason 34
Dialectic of Enlightenment 5, 77,
    126

differentiation
    functional differentiation 9, 20,
        21, 22, 23, 24, 32
    rationalization and 9, 22, 34,
        53, 55, 56, 57, 58
    social differentiation 53–4
Dilthey, Wilhelm 16, 81
discourse 18, 40, 103
    action and 42, 95
    consensus and 48
    ethical-moral discourse 48,
        116, 121
    legal discourse 48, 97, 116
    of modernity 68, 77–8, 154
    participants in 83
    political participation 134, 136
    practical discourse 44, 45, 46
    principle of 48
    public discourse 125, 132
    rational discourse 96, 98, 109,
        127
    structure of 38
    theoretical discourse 46
    types of 16
    validity in 86
discourse ethics 43–7, 100–21,
        129
    argumentation 106–7, 116–17,
        119
    moral theory 104–14
    system of practical discourses
        114–21
discourse principle (D) 44, 45
discourse theory 53, 79, 121,
        127, 133
    of law 104, 129
    of truth 94–8
Döbert, Rainer 105
Droysen, Johann Gustav 81
Dummett, Michael 8, 18, 39, 41,
        84, 85, 94, 95
Durkheim, Émile 21, 102

Eastern Europe 138
Eckhart, Meister 173n.12

Einstein, Albert 158
Engels, Friedrich 130
enlightenment
    dialectic of 72
    philosophy and 147, 148–9
    self-enlightenment 153
epistemic rationality 29, 38,
        87
epistemology 8, 99, 164
    reconstructive epistemology 17,
        18, 30, 33–5, 50
ethical life
    morality and 105, 110, 111
ethical-moral discourse 48, 116,
        121
European neo-conservatism 25
European Union 139, 144,
        204n.13
    nationalist movements 138–9
evidence theory of truth 96

facticity
    validity and 63, 126, 135, 136
fallibilism/fallibility 13, 14, 15,
        31, 34, 43, 124, 153, 156
Feuerbach, Ludwig 149
formal pragmatics 22, 36–7, 41,
        64–5, 66–7, 69, 72, 80–6
    communicative action 69,
        92
    the lifeworld 69–70
    rational acceptability 87
    theory of meaning 80–6, 91
    theory of truth 96–7
Forsthoff, Ernst 202n.5
frames of reference 15, 23, 25,
        27, 48, 50
    definition 20
Frankfurt School 5, 11–12, 25,
        33, 60, 182n.63
    see also Institute for Social
        Research
free will 115, 118, 166
freedom 108, 150
    of choice 115

communicative freedoms 137, 138
equal freedom 139
individual freedoms 113
Kant on 115
political freedom 137
public and private autonomy 53, 55, 128, 136–7, 150
to say no 109
Frege, Gottlob 36, 39, 81, 83, 89, 94
Freyer, Hans 125

Gadamer, Hans-Georg 4, 5, 6, 12, 14, 34, 36, 47
meaning 65
prejudices 7
Truth and Method 60
Gauss Lectures 17, 19, 31, 32, 39, 40, 60, 62, 65, 68, 69, 95
Gehlen, Arnold 4, 7, 49, 125, 127–8
German Historical School 81
German Marxism *see* Marxism
German philosophy 4, 148
idealism 25, 35, 55, 56, 159, 164
pre-war 4, 5, 6, 122–3, 151–2
German Platonic tradition 7, 19
German Romanticism 6–7, 35, 56, 57
Germany 26, 100, 125
catch-up revolution 11
denazification 122–3
Federal Republic of Germany (FRG) 3, 4, 6, 122, 123
German Democratic Republic (GDR) 3, 4, 5
post-war intellectual landscape 3–4, 5, 6–7, 81, 148
re-education 3, 6, 11–12
Weimar period 127
see also National Socialism/ Nazism
Gulf Wars 55, 142

Haller, Michael 142, 155
Hegel, G.W.F. 5, 61, 71, 72, 76–7, 148
absolute spirit 149
dialectic of reason 34
Kant and 108
morality 108, 110
philosophy of right 126, 128
postmetaphysical thinking 156
religion and 164, 165, 166
Hegelianism 27, 37, 46, 52, 61
Hegelian Marxism 4–5, 8, 9, 12, 25, 27
Left Hegelianism 56
Right Hegelianism 4, 7, 43, 100, 127
Young Hegelians 5, 149, 155, 156
Heidegger, Martin 4, 7, 34, 36, 56, 77, 81, 82, 83, 99, 151
Henrich, Dieter 157–8
Herder, Johann Gottfried 149, 172n.12
hermeneutic tradition 4, 6
hermeneutic turn 6, 8, 9, 26, 42, 57
historian's debate 26
historical materialism 35, 55–6
Hobbes, Thomas 55, 112, 122, 164
Horkheimer, Max 12, 33, 34, 57
Critical Theory 126
critique of reason 79
Dialectic of Enlightenment 5
dialectic of reason 34
Marxism 8
human rights 51, 53, 55, 155
international law 143–5
religion and 167
Humboldt, Wilhelm von 6, 36, 60, 81, 83, 149
Hume, David 39, 93, 159
Husserl, Edmund 58, 62, 69, 71, 161

ideology
  Marxist critique 9, 56, 149
illocutionary force 31
illocutionary goal/success 39, 64,
    85, 90–1
illocutionary speech acts 66–7, 106
indigenous peoples 140
inferential semantics 64, 86
Institute for Social Research 125,
    175n.20, 176n.25
  see also Frankfurt School
instrumental action 14, 15–16,
    22, 37, 41
instrumental rationality 29, 33,
    72, 101
interactive competence 44, 53,
    105
  see also communicative
    competence
international law 54–5, 141–5

Jasper, Karl 169
justification
  of moral principle 107–8
  of norms of action 108–9
  truth and 26, 29, 40–3, 48,
    96–7
justified assertability 18, 29, 97,
    98

Kant, Immanuel 16, 18, 27, 39,
    43, 61, 83, 102, 110, 122,
    148
  categorical imperative 106
  constructivism 47, 112
  Critique of Practical Reason 8
  deontology 98
  dialectic of reason 34
  on freedom/free will 115
  Hegel and 108
  metaphysics 48–9, 156, 160
  moral theory 46, 48–9, 76
  moral use of practical reason
    48
  perpetual peace 54

philosophy of law 143
postmetaphysical thinking 156,
    157, 158, 160
pragmatism 82, 99, 100
public opinion 14
religion and 164, 165, 166
Religion within the Boundaries
    of Mere Reason 59
self-education 8
self-enlightenment 153
theory of ideas 94
What is Enlightenment? 8
Keynesian economics 3, 126,
    177n.27
Kleine politische Schriften 22, 123
Knowledge and Human Interests
    16, 18, 35, 60, 61, 99, 150
Kohlberg, Lawrence 20, 33, 46,
    75, 105
Koselleck, Reinhart 177n.26,
    203n.6

Lafont, Christina 98
law 23, 48
  common law 136
  constitutional law 77, 125,
    127, 137
  discourse theory of 104, 129
  Hegel on 126
  international law 54–5, 141–5
  legitimacy of 135–7
  moral law 166
  morality and 29, 48, 76, 115,
    121, 136
  objective laws 128
  philosophy of 28, 121, 126,
    143
  positive law 136, 137
  rational law 76
  Rawl's theory of justice 45, 46,
    47, 49, 112
  rule of law 49, 50, 51, 53, 127,
    135, 136, 137
  theory of 11, 27, 29, 46, 49–55
learning 53–5

Left Hegelianism 56
legal discourse 48, 97, 116
legal systems 74, 136
legitimacy 32, 102, 132, 135–7
Leninism 12, 14
Levinas, Emmanuel 111
liberalism 51–2, 153
  concept of justice 112
  liberal models of democracy 52,
    133
  liberal rationalism 4
lifeworld 58, 69–73, 99
  colonization of 33, 49–50, 73
  communicative action and 68,
    69, 70, 73, 160–3
  communicative rationality 91–3
  naturalism and 160–3
  rationalization of 72
  reproduction of 32
linguistic competence 66, 79
linguistic turn 6, 8, 9, 26, 35, 39,
    43, 57, 60, 79, 83
linguistic understanding 82, 84–6
Locke, John 51
logocentrism 10, 159
Lorenz, Kuno 100
Lorenzen, Paul 98, 100
Löwith, Karl 9, 12, 14, 55, 149
  From Hegel to Nietzsche 4, 5,
    148
Luhmann, Niklas 8, 22, 49, 128,
    131
Lukács, Georg 9, 12, 25, 33, 34,
    76, 151
  German Marxism 4–5, 8
  *History and Class
    Consciousness* 5, 61

McCarthy, Thomas 92
Machiavelli, Niccolò 14
MacIntyre, A. 44
Marcuse, Herbert 7, 8, 33
Marx, Karl 12, 13, 56, 76, 148,
    149
  Communist Manifesto 130

  dialectic of reason 34
  positivism 14
  self-reflection of history 149–50
  theory of surplus value 61
Marxism 12–14, 52, 127
  Austro-Marxism 176n.25,
    202n.4
  critical Marxism 11, 26
  critique of ideology 9, 56,
    149–50
  critiques of modernity 34
  German Marxism 4–5, 8, 9, 25
  Hegelian Marxism 4–5, 8, 9,
    12, 25, 27
  social action model 14
  Weberian Marxism 4–5, 8, 9,
    12, 25, 27, 33, 75
  Western Marxism 75
mass culture 13, 14, 16, 24–5
Max Planck Institute, Starnberg
    16, 19, 25, 102, 105, 153,
    191n.19, 195n.3
Mead, George Herbert 15, 20,
    33, 65, 120
  intersubjectivity 71–2
meaning 58, 65
  discourse theory of truth 94–8,
    121
  formal pragmatics 80–6, 91
  normative dimension of 40
  philosophical meaning 148
  production of 63
  reason and 40
  sociological meaning 9
  theory of 28, 35, 36–7, 67,
    79–94
meaning structures 63–4
metaphysics
  destiny of being 81
  Kantian 48–9, 156, 160
  philosophical substantialism 7
  post-Kantian 157–8
  postmetaphysical thinking and
    5, 14, 164
  religion and 158, 161, 164, 165

Michelman, Frank 137
modernity 24, 31, 33–5, 58
  critique of 77
  dialectic of 24, 33
  discourse of 68, 77–8, 154
  German idealism and 25
  German Platonic tradition and
    7
  philosophical discourse of 68
  religion and 168
  self-understanding of 77–8,
    148, 153
  solidarity movements 140–1
monotheism 114
morality
  deontological morality 115
  ethical life and 105, 110, 111
  happiness and 165–6
  Hegel on 108, 110
  law and 29, 48, 76, 115, 121,
    136
  meaning of 117, 118, 120
  rational morality 113, 166
  realist conceptions of 106
  religion and 166
  theory of 27, 101, 104, 117
  universalist morality 47, 105,
    112
multiculturalism 140
Münster School 126
myth 16, 21, 23

Nagel, Thomas 145
nation state 142, 144, 145
National Socialism/Nazism 3, 4,
    11, 43, 49, 122
  denazification 122–3
  nationalism and 123, 124, 125
  re-education 3, 6, 11–12
  the Volk 124, 125
national sovereignty 55, 131
nationalism 54
  Nazi ideology 123, 124, 125
  Western Europe 138–9
natural science 14, 57, 65, 162

naturalism 57–8, 160–4
neo-conservatism 7, 25, 55
neo-republicanism 7
neo-structuralists 7
neural materialism 8, 58
Nielsen, Torben Hviid 110
Nietzsche, Friedrich 111, 173n.12
Nunner-Winkler, Gertrud 105

Oevermann, Ulrich 104
On the Logic of the Social
    Sciences 15, 17, 60, 65

Parsons, Talcott 8, 15, 20, 22,
    33, 149
Peace of Westphalia 1684 142
Peirce, Charles Sanders 6, 8, 10,
    14, 16, 42, 43, 60, 82, 95
perlocutionary success 39
philosophical anthropology 4, 5,
    9, 18
philosophy 146–69
  democracy and 155–6
  enlightenment 147, 148–9
  metaphilosophical reflections
    151–6
  postmetaphysical see
    postmetaphysical thinking
  reflection 147–8
  religion and 146
  science and 146–8, 152–5, 164
  secularization 152–3
  self-understanding 147–8, 154
Piaget, Jean 33, 42, 105, 210n.20
Plato 146, 172n.12
Plessner, Helmuth 4
Popper, Karl 4, 5, 7–8, 12, 14, 34,
    82, 101
popular sovereignty 53, 131,
    133–4, 136
positive law 136, 137
positivism 7–8, 14, 25
postmetaphysical thinking 5, 8,
    10, 26, 56, 57, 59, 76, 154,
    156–60

constitutional principles 138
metaphysics and 5, 14, 164
naturalism and 161–3
religion and 164, 167, 168
postmodernism 27, 35, 42, 55,
    78, 112–13
practical discourse 44, 45, 46
pragmatic turn 6, 8, 9, 26, 42, 57
pragmatism 42–3
    American pragmatism 6, 71
    communicative action 67, 69
    Kantian pragmatism 82, 99, 100
    language and 67, 80, 87, 94,
        157
    Peircean pragmatism 6, 8
    pragmatic presuppositions 42,
        44, 92–3, 96, 120
    pragmatic use of reason 47
    transcendental pragmatics 82,
        100
    universal pragmatics 17, 23, 32
    uses of reason 114, 115
primitive society 15–16, 20, 21
public discourse 125, 132
public opinion 12, 14, 52, 132,
    134
public sphere 12, 13, 16, 50, 52
    civil society 126, 132
    democracy and 132, 134
    dialectic of 19, 23–4, 35
    philosophy and 154
    religion in 141
    Schmittian school 127
    transformation of 125
Putnam, Hilary 42, 97, 99, 163

Quine, Willard Van Orman 18,
    35, 81, 99

rational choice theory 77
rational discourse 96, 98, 109,
    127
rationality, theory of 79–94
    communicative rationality
        33–4, 37–8, 72, 86–94, 111

rationalization 33, 127, 129
    differentiation and 9, 22, 34,
        53, 55, 56, 57, 58
    of the lifeworld 72
    social rationalization 68, 72,
        73
    Western modernization 77
Rawls, John 27, 113
    Theory of Justice 44, 100
    theory of justice 45, 46, 47, 49,
        112
re-education 122–3
    see also denazification
realist turn 40, 47, 48, 52
reasoned discourse 17
reconstructive epistemology 17,
    18, 30, 33–5, 50
religion 47, 58–9, 164–9
    Christian tradition 164, 165
    constitutional state and 137–41
    human rights and 167
    Judeo-Christian tradition 113,
        152, 167
    metaphysics and 158, 161, 164,
        165
    monotheism 114
    philosophy and 146
    postmetaphysical thinking and
        164, 167, 168
    return of 57
    secularization and 164, 166,
        167, 168, 169
    truth and 164
Renner, Karl 202n.4
republicanism 7
    classical republicanism 131
    models of democracy 52, 133
    neo-republicanism 7
Riedel, Manfred 100
Right Hegelianism 4, 7, 43, 100,
    127
rightness claims 29, 42, 44, 67,
    85, 98, 117, 118, 119, 120
Ritter, Joachim 4, 7, 43, 126,
    128

Romanticism 7, 8, 25, 35
    German Romanticism 6–7, 56,
        57
Rorty, Richard 27, 35, 41, 42, 97
Rosenberg, Alfred 173n.12
Rothacker, Erich 4, 60, 81
Rousseau, Jean-Jacques 51, 122
rule of law 49, 50, 51, 53, 127,
        135, 136, 137

Scheler, Max 5
Schelling, Friedrich Wilhelm
        Joseph 171n.7, 210n.20
Schelsky, Helmut 126, 128, 148
Schiller, Friedrich 8
Schleiermacher, Friedrich 81
Schmitt, Carl 4, 7, 49, 55, 125,
        127, 128, 151
Schnädelbach, Herbert 87
Schulz, Walter 95
Schumpeter, Joseph 131
Schütz, Alfred 8, 15, 17, 62
science
    history of 73–4
    natural science 14, 57, 65, 162
    naturalism 57–8, 160–4
    neural materialism 8, 58
    philosophy and 146–8, 152–5,
        164
    self-understanding of 58
Searle, John 8, 95
    speech act theory 17, 66–7, 69,
        79, 84
secularization
    of philosophy 152–3
    religion and 164, 166, 167,
        168, 169
    self-understanding 164
    of state power 138, 140, 141
self-determination 53, 54, 139,
        141
self-education 8
self-enlightenment 153
self-reflection 18, 61, 149–50,
        151

self-regulating system 131
self-understanding 75, 158, 160,
        161
    ethical self-understanding 115
    of modernity 77–8, 148, 153
    philosophy and 147–8, 154
    of the present 149
    of science 58
    secular self-understanding 164
    'self' of 147, 148
Sellars, Wilfrid 86
Simitis, Spiros 127
Simmel, Georg 62
social action 57, 67, 68–9, 80, 91
    Marxist model 14
    symbolic dimensions 31, 34
    see also communicative action
social contract theory 164
social Darwinism 143
social differentiation 53–4
social evolution 23, 73, 110, 150
social integration 23, 50, 70, 73
social order 32, 67, 68, 69
social pathologies 62, 72
sovereignty
    international law 143–4
    popular sovereignty 53, 131,
        133–4, 136
Soviet Union 138
speech acts
    illocutionary force 31
    illocutionary goal/success 39,
        64, 85, 90–1
    illocutionary speech acts 66–7,
        106
    reaching mutual understanding
        64, 66, 67, 68, 79–80, 83,
        85, 87–92
    Searle's theory of 17, 66–7, 69,
        79, 84
    validity claims 17–18, 31, 37,
        38, 39
Spinoza, Baruch 164
Starnberg Institute see Max
        Planck Institute, Starnberg

Strachey, John 202n.4
strategic action 15–16, 22, 37
Strawson, Peter F. 95, 106
structuralism 64, 105
  neo-structuralists 7
Studienausgabe 17, 26, 27, 29
substantialism 7, 8, 9, 43, 45, 49
subsystems 125, 126, 128, 131,
    134
system
  concept of 70
  functionalist systems theory 77
  legal systems 74, 136
  self-regulating 131
system functionalism 128
system of rules
  of communication 31
  grammatical rules 64
systemic integration 23, 50, 69,
    70
systemic rationality 72
systems theory 8, 49, 77

Tanner Lectures 51, 129
Taylor, Charles 44, 46
*Technik und Wissenschaft als
    Ideologie* 15, 19
technocracy 7, 14, 16, 24–5, 128
technocratic state 13, 24, 125
  post-war Germany 3
technological progress 14, 129,
    152
theoretical discourse 46
Theory of Communicative Action
    12, 20, 24, 49, 50, 72, 80,
    105, 151, 155
Toulmin, Stephen 8, 17, 41, 67,
    98
transcendental pragmatics 82,
    100
truth
  consensus theory of 18, 67, 95,
    96–7, 98
  correspondence theory of 35,
    40–2, 79, 95

discourse theory of 94–8
  evidence theory of 96
  immanent reference to 62, 63
  justification and 26, 29, 40–3,
    48, 96–7
  religion and 164, 167
  theories of 11, 18, 40–3, 46, 80
  truth conditions 89–90
  validity claims *see* validity
    claims
truth semantics 84, 85
truthfulness claims 67, 85, 90, 91

understanding
  Gadamer's theory of 7
  linguistic understanding 82,
    84–6
  objectivity of 74
  reaching mutual understanding
    64, 66, 67, 68, 79–80, 83,
    85, 87–92
  reconstructive understanding
    33–4, 75
  speech acts 39
United Nations 142–5
universal pragmatics 17, 23, 32
universalization principle (U)
    44–5, 100, 107, 108, 118

validity
  deontic validity 102, 117
  in discourse 86
  facticity and 63, 126, 135, 136
  meaning and 84
  of norms 45, 48, 98, 102, 108
  theory of 40–1
validity claims 17–18, 22–3, 29,
    30–5, 41–2, 48, 63–4, 66–7,
    68, 69, 70, 84–6, 117, 158
  argumentation 87–8
  communicative rationality
    86–94
  context-transcending claims 40
  discursive redemption of 67,
    87, 104

validity claims (*cont.*)
  legal validity 104, 144
  moral validity 98, 101, 104,
    106, 110, 112, 114, 117
  normative claims 103, 104,
    106, 108, 135
  of reason 157
  rightness claims 29, 42, 44, 67,
    85, 98, 117, 118, 119, 120
  of speech acts 17–18, 31, 37,
    38, 39
  truth claims 18, 29, 35, 42, 67,
    85, 87, 96, 98
  truthfulness claims 67, 85, 90,
    91
values 47, 115, 120
Vico, Giambattista 14
Vienna Circle 4, 57

Walzer, Michael 44
Weber, Max 8, 15, 33, 34, 49,
    65, 76
  dialectic of reason 34
  ideal types 15

legal systems 74
social rationalization 68, 72, 73
social theory 15
value spheres 154
Weber, Werner 202n.5
Weberian Marxism 4–5, 8, 9, 12,
    25, 27, 33, 75
Weisberber, Leo 60
Wellmer, Albrecht 82, 98
Winckelmann, Johann Joachim
    173n.12
Wittgenstein, Ludwig 6, 8, 14,
    17, 36
  critique of modernity 77
  language games 15, 82–3
  meaning 65
  Philosophical Investigations 60,
    81
World Congress of the
    International Association for
    Media and Communications
    Research 133

Young Hegelians 5, 149, 155, 156